Sometime in Napa
Valley — Saith by Some
+
They all lived happily ever
after!

Carol + Daniel
1994

LA CASA SENA

THE CUISINE OF SANTA FE

GORDON HEISS
&
JOHN HARRISSON

Ten Speed Press
Berkeley, California

TEN SPEED PRESS
P.O. Box 7123
Berkeley, CA 94707

Cover and text design by Fifth Street Design, Berkeley, California. Photography by Lois Ellen Frank, Santa Fe, New Mexico.

Product names mentioned herein may be legally protected trademarks and/or registered trademarks of their respective companies. It is not our intent to use any of these names generically.

Library of Congress Cataloging-in Publication Data
Heiss, Gordon.
    La Casa Sena : the cuisine of Santa Fe / by Gordon Heiss and
John Harrisson.
        p.   cm.
    Includes index.
    ISBN 0-89815-565-7
    1. La Casa Sena (Restaurant) 2. Cookery, American—Southwestern style.
    3. Cookery— New Mexico— Santa Fe.   I. Harrisson, John. II. Title.
TX715.2.S69H45   1994
641.59789—dc20   94-6335
                                                                        CIP

FIRST PRINTING 1994

Printed in the United States of America
1   2   3   4   5 — 98   97   96   95   94

Table of Contents

List of Recipes

Breakfast, Brunch & Lunch

Breads

Appetizers

Soups & Stews

Salads & Dressings

Fish & Seafood

The Art of La Casa Sena

*Opposite page:
The patio of Sena Plaza
looking at La Casa Sena
ca. 1935. Photo by
T. Harmon Parkhurst.
Courtesy Museum of
New Mexico.*

The Story of La Casa Sena

BIEN VENIDA

La Casa Sena has been described as "one of the finest and most atmospheric restaurants in the Southwest." We are proud of our reputation and the popularity we enjoy in Santa Fe. Our clientele, both local and from out of town, makes us feel very much appreciated, and without all of these people, of course, there would be no restaurant and no cookbook. With this collection of recipes, we acknowledge all those who have made La Casa Sena an institution in Santa Fe; we are grateful for your patronage and support over the years.

Many come not just for the food but also to admire our renowned collection of Southwestern museum-quality art. More than seventy pieces grace the walls, and some are featured in the Cantina, an informal dining room that adjoins the restaurant and shares its high standards. Here, service is provided by troubadours — trained singers, actors, and performers — who sing selections from the musical theater while guests enjoy the delicious Southwestern cuisine.

During the summer, another attraction is the opportunity to sit outside and admire the flowering bushes and beautiful trees of the Sena Plaza Courtyard and the historic building dating back to the middle of the last century that La Casa Sena has occupied since 1983. In fact, the Sena Plaza is one of the oldest surviving houses in the city and certainly one of the most attractive. In the heart of Santa Fe, the restaurant is just one block away from the city's Plaza — the end of the legendary Santa Fe Trail — and the same distance from another landmark, the Saint Francis Cathedral.

La Casa Sena occupies a fine old *hacienda*-style adobe complex and means "the Sena House." The Sena family was one of the oldest and most notable in Santa Fe. The founder of the family, Bernadino de Sena, was an orphan from Mexico City who traveled to Santa Fe in 1693. His skills as a craftsman made him wealthy by frontier standards. The family continued the crafts and blacksmithing tradition well into the nineteenth century and became prominent members of Santa Fe's community. The land on which their *casa* was built was originally property granted to Captain Arias de Quiros by General Diego de Vargas, who reconquered Santa Fe for the Spanish in 1693. The property was deeded through the family to Maria del Rosario Alarid, the wife of Juan Sena, and then to their son, Major José Sena. In 1864, Major Sena married Doña Isabel Cabeza de Baca, who came from another prominent Santa Fe family. With the land came a small adobe house, built in 1831, and it was this structure that Major Sena extended into a thirty-three-room hacienda in 1868 when New Mexico was still a territory of the United States. (Statehood was not to follow for more than forty years.)

Isabel had already made a good start on producing the family's twenty-two children (only eleven of whom were born alive), so even this large house did not have a lot of rooms to spare. It was here that the Major, a social lion of the city, entertained the VIPs of the day, from long-forgotten governors and dignitaries to well-remembered individuals such as the frontiersman Kit Carson. Even then, the establishment offered the finest cuisine of the region. Venison, rabbit, buffalo, and all manner of game fowl were served together with the agricultural produce of the vicinity, including the ubiquitous chiles. At the Sena house, the legendary Spanish hospitality extended to include day-long feasts, with sports, games, and dancing.

A ballroom on the second floor of the west wing of the house was filled with merriment and song. It temporarily became the territory of New Mexico's legislative chamber in 1892 when the original capitol burned in a fire. The property also included a chicken house, coach house, servants' quarters, storerooms on the northern side, and two wells, one of which is still in use. The courtyard, now the most lush garden in the area, was then bare earth and the goats ate anything that started to grow; plants that required water and labor were for human consumption. This marvelous compound was as close to luxury as one could imagine in the rigorous days of frontier life. The stables were where the main dining room of La Casa Sena is now.

After Major Sena and his wife died, the land was divided among the six surviving children. In 1927, these heirs deeded the building to Senator Bronson Cutting and two sisters, Martha and Amelia White. With other tenants they set about renovating the grand old home. A tea room was built in the stables, a second floor added to the east wing, and all the rooms became either stores or offices. One of these offices was used in the 1940s as the headquarters for the Manhattan Project, which later developed the atomic bomb in nearby Los Alamos.

In the early 1980s, the ravages of time finally began to take a toll. An art dealer, Gerald Peters, bought this historic building and extensively renovated it without making any architectural changes. The restoration succeeded in keeping the historic ambiance and integrity of the Sena Plaza intact. La Casa Sena opened in the space that the tea room had occupied years earlier. Merriment and song once again filled the old house that had belonged to Major Sena. And again the great indigenous cuisine of the region enthralled its visitors.

Palace Avenue circa 1920 with Sena Plaza in the background. A portal was added to Sena Plaza in the late '20s.

The Story of Santa Fe

The American Southwest has a long and illustrious history. Continuous human habitation in the region predates the first Spanish settlements by many centuries, and successive native American cultures, including those of the Hohokam, Mogollon, and Anasazi, have been established here since at least the first century A.D. In the fifteenth and sixteenth centuries, the agrarian Pueblo Indians settled in communities along the Rio Grande valley. To the west, the Zuni and Hopi flourished. These people grew corn, beans, squash, and chiles and developed an extensive trading network with other Indian groups to the east as well as to the south, in Mexico.

The first Spanish expeditions from Mexico to the American Southwest set out in the 1540s to find legendary hoards of gold and treasure. Santa Fe (La Villa Real de Santa Fe de San Francisco de Assisi is its original name) was founded in 1610 as the capital of the region (thus becoming the first capital city in the present United States), and the Palace of the Governors, which still stands in the city's Plaza, was being built ten years before the Pilgrims landed at Plymouth Rock. Santa Fe marked the northern terminus of the Camino Real, the trade route that ran south to Mexico City. Its existence did much to facilitate Spanish colonization.

Decades of Spanish oppression led to the Pueblo Revolt of 1680, perhaps the most effective action ever mounted by Native Americans in the New World against outside forces. The Spanish withdrew from the region but returned in 1692 under the leadership of General Diego de Vargas. A period of steady colonization followed, and missions, garrisons (or *presidios*), and civilian settlements were established. The Indians and the Spanish coexisted in relative peace over the following decades.

When Mexico won its independence from Spain in 1821, the Southwest came under the rule of its neighbor to the south. In the same year, when Santa Fe was still a community of about five thousand inhabitants, the famous trade route, the Santa Fe Trail, was opened up from Missouri eight hundred miles to the east, and the English-speaking influence in the region grew steadily.

In 1846, the United States claimed the region and, after the two-year Mexican War, New Mexico became a U.S. territory in 1850. There then followed a tremendous immigration of Anglo pioneers, soldiers, and traders from the east, and a network of military forts was set up to protect the territory from Indian raids and Confederate forces during the Civil War. The distinctive tricultural heritage of Santa Fe and New Mexico — the native American, Spanish, and Anglo — was forged during this period.

It was a time when boom-and-bust gold and silver rushes were beginning and frontier lawlessness was common. Life in Santa Fe at the time was certainly colorful. Reports from merchants, soldiers, and others who traveled from the East described the population as consisting of men who all smoked (and, worse, the women did too), rampant gambling on cards and cockfights, and fandangos every night. Descriptions of Santa Fe during the 1800s were scarcely flattering: "a prairie-dog town," said one; another (the explorer and general Zebulon Pike) described the populace as "a lazy gossiping people always lounging on their blankets and smoking cigarillos." An account by one trader in the 1840s reported that "the houses were nearly all dilapidated, the streets narrow and filthy, and the people, when in best attire, not half dressed."

The mid-1800s saw the appointment of the Frenchman, Archbishop Lamy, to the diocese of Santa Fe, and he inaugurated the building of the Romanesque Cathedral of Saint Francis across from Sena Plaza. During this period too, hospitals and schools were founded in the city.

The Civil War touched Santa Fe (as it did La Casa Sena — the Major served in the fighting). Confederate troops from Texas seized public buildings in early 1862. The Governor fled. On March 26, Confederate and Union troops clashed at Glorieta Pass, fifteen miles east of Santa Fe. Confederate losses forced a retreat, but New Mexico remained under martial law until the end of the war.

After the Civil War, Santa Fe became a focal point of trade and thus relatively prosperous. There was "a good comfortable spring carriage" that traveled to El Paso every other month on the Camino Real (though how they made it up or down the steep La Bajada hill just outside Santa Fe remains a mystery), and wagon trains traveled regularly along the Old Santa Fe Trail bringing a variety of goods, from bathtubs to brocades from Europe and Mexico. The bustling town would stop for siesta between one and three in the afternoon, and at twilight the bells would toll for vespers; residents stopped whatever they were doing to observe a two-minute silence. Later, in the 1880s, the railroad reached El Paso and then New Mexico, giving the interior access to both coasts, an event that was to transform the life-style and economy of the entire Southwest, linking it to the rest of the country. In 1912 New Mexico was granted statehood as the forty-seventh state in the Union.

San Francisco Street looking east. Courtesy Museum of New Mexico.

At La Casa Sena

The Southwestern cuisine served at La Casa Sena draws on the rich history of the region. When we were devising the menu before we first opened, we researched the city's history library for countless hours to determine which foods might have been served on special occasions during the heyday of Major Sena's great house. When changing the menu, we still ask ourselves: "What would Major Sena have served, had he owned an airplane?" We should hasten to explain that the reference to the airplane is an acknowledgment of modern expeditious food distribution — a "Back-to-the-Future" equation for La Casa Sena.

We attach great importance to the acquisition of the finest seasonal ingredients. Even the restaurant's water comes from a private well. For fresh produce, especially the chiles, our suppliers are preferably local growers, and, where we can, we use indigenous ingredients. For example, La Casa Sena's distinctive red chile is grown for the restaurant near Dixon, on the Rio Grande in northern New Mexico. The harsh weather there means that this local product is not plentiful and, because the restaurant purchases virtually the entire crop, it is unlikely that this chile will be tasted anywhere else in the world.

The Southwestern cuisine we serve is complex and eclectic, in part because of the diverse origins of the recipes. The cuisine of this region is based on many influences: the native American, the Mexican, the Hispanic, and various waves of European immigration. In addition, our food is the product of a number of different people who have brought their talents to the kitchen, wine cellar, and bar.

The late Leslie Fargen was the opening chef of La Casa Sena, and his enduring contributions, melding Spanish and Pueblo Indian cultures, stemmed from the Santa Fe heritage of which he was rightly proud. He liked to claim that his forebears were attending an Inaugural Ball for the Governor in Santa Fe on the very day that the Pilgrims were landing at Plymouth Rock.

Many of our sauces were developed and contributed by another heir to the original Spanish culture in Santa Fe, Alonzo Archuleta. Chef Kip McClerin, a graduate of the Culinary Institute of America, became a specialist in the art of cooking with chiles and built the restaurant's chile larder to an amazing twenty-two varieties. He used them in a compelling manner with recipes that have become a permanent part of our repertoire. David Jones, who apprenticed in France and was a sous-chef at the Tavern on the Green in New York City before moving West, added a more eclectic Southwestern element to the menu while he was executive chef.

Ambjörn Lindskog began his culinary reign at La Casa Sena in 1992 and has woven his magic into virtually every aspect of the restaurant's menu and recipes. Ambjörn was a nuclear scientist in his native Sweden before he came to the United States. He had long planned to switch careers to the arts partway through his life, and he followed his love and talent for cooking to a logical conclusion. He opened a catering business in California and served such notables as China's Prime Minister Li Peng and the late Andrei Sakharov. He studied in France under the chef Marc Meneau before working as sous-chef at The Pierre in Manhattan. Ambjörn moved back to California where he was executive chef at 231 Ellsworth in San Mateo, and then he took up the reins here at La Casa Sena.

Kelly Rogers, who joined us as executive chef in 1994, is a philosophy graduate, which qualifies him to give our food and menu deep thought. Kelly honed his skills in his native state of Oklahoma before progressing through the ranks at our firstrate Santa Fe restaurants such as Cafe Pasqual's, Coyote Cafe, and SantaCafe. This background gives him a unique perspective on all aspects of Southwestern cuisine.

The pastry chef Patrick Levesque has contributed some of the bread and dessert recipes. Patrick served his apprenticeship in his native France and, after moving to the United States, spent several years at Wolfgang Puck's Postrio restaurant in San Francisco.

No description of the culinary evolution at La Casa Sena would be complete without mentioning our impressive collection of wine. Our list has received *The Wine Spectator* award for many years. We started out with a whopping 150 selections, and this has grown to more than seven hundred with the help and expertise of Deborah Magid, Jill Cashman, Deborah Kerr, Meg Hayes, and lastly Greg Grissom. The philosophy behind the choice of wines we carry is simple: They should be appropriate to the food. Almost all our wine comes from the United States, France, and Spain.

We also serve private-label Chardonnay and Pinot Noir wines. Private-label wines are usually purchased after they have been made. However, La Casa Sena's are made from grapes that the restaurant buys and has crushed, fermented, pressed, aged, and bottled by wineries and winemakers who are happy to rent their facilities to us. The results have been outstanding. Some of our house bottles are adorned by spectacular labels designed by artists, among them Georgia O'Keeffe, Helen Frankenthaler, Wayne Thiebaud and Paul Wonner.

The noble pursuit of mixology is also honored at La Casa Sena. And you will find scattered among the following pages some of our most popular libations. They are particularly delicious with appetizers or at brunch, or even instead of dessert.

The restaurant is also an art gallery. Our guests often ask about the spectacular collection of artwork that hangs on the walls. Some of these paintings are reproduced in the photographs illustrating this book; another is on the cover. La Casa Sena houses a portion of the collection, assembled by Gerald Peters, of paintings by artists who are recognized as having been part of the art colony that arose in Santa Fe in the first half of the twentieth century. Few groups of artists have existed as long or claimed as many permanent residents as did the colonies in Northern New Mexico. The Taos Society of Artists, established in the early 1900s, was soon followed in Santa Fe by groups calling themselves The New Mexican Painters and *Los Cincos Pintores*.

Beginning with an interest in the art of the American West, Mr. Peters built up a collection comprising the finest paintings of artists from Taos and Santa Fe and the work of classical Western painters and sculptors. With galleries in Santa Fe, Dallas, and New York, Mr. Peters has expanded his scope and now also exhibits American Impressionists and modern artists, sculptors, and photographers. The entire art collection at La Casa Sena is a permanent exhibit and has remained virtually unchanged since 1984. An equally distinguished collection of Native American art, also assembled by Gerald Peters, hangs in the Cantina adjoining the restaurant.

That's not the only attraction in the Cantina, however. There our customers are served by trained singers and actors and entertained every night of the year except for Christmas by their unforgettable performances

Evening Shadows
Theodore Van Soelen

Dry Wash
Arthur Haddock

Near San Ildefonso
Sheldon Parsons

of Broadway show tunes. The occasional aria compensates opera-lovers during the ten months of the year the town's opera company is closed.

Only singers with considerable theater experience and/or a degree in music or drama are invited to audition for the Cantina Troubadours. The general policy proclaims, "If they can carry a tune, we'll teach them to carry a tray." But most applicants admit that there are few in the performing arts who haven't waited tables at one time or another! Many take the job because of the extensive training we offer, and not just in customer service. Our coaches also teach them voice, music, acting, and dancing.

In the best tradition of Major Sena, the merrymaking in the Cantina is overseen by our musical director, Mark Parker. But it is, perhaps, Greg Grissom who has the strangest job description in any restaurant: manager of the Cantina; buyer of the huge, prestigious wine list; and lead baritone. His voice has such depth that he is one of the major performers in Santa Fe Opera's pre-season school program and his renditions from *Phantom of the Opera* are acclaimed far and wide.

With beautiful art, good tunes, and outstanding food and drink, La Casa Sena is a feast for all the senses.

Greg Grissom stands on the bar in the Cantina to sing Phantom of the Opera.

Portal, Sena Plaza ca. 1920. Courtesy Museum of New Mexico.

Breakfast, Brunch, & Lunch

*F*or the first five years La Casa Sena was open, we served breakfast, but then we decided to concentrate on serving lunch during the week and brunch on the weekends, as well as dinner. Many of the items on the old breakfast menu were, however, classics and remain brunch favorites.

The distinction between brunch and lunch is equally hazy, as it probably should be. History is instructive in this regard. Brunch is said to have been "invented" in New Orleans toward the end of the last century, when enterprising eateries offered "second breakfasts" to shopworkers and tradesmen after their early morning custom had slackened off. These second breakfasts were, in effect, early lunches and so the hybrid, brunch, was born.

This chapter has a distinctive Southwestern flavor to it (regional dishes such as *burritos* are particularly popular for breakfast and brunch in Santa Fe). Some recipes included here can be adapted for dinner; others, particularly the sandwiches, can equally well be prepared as snacks or as picnic food, an attractive versatility of much Southwestern food.

It's not unusual to see a look of bewilderment cross the faces of new visitors to the Southwest when they order burritos or *enchiladas* for breakfast or lunch and are immediately asked by their waiter, "Red or green?" The question refers to the preferred color of chile sauce that is to accompany the dish. It is perfectly proper to order both, in which case the correct reply is, "Christmas." The more sophisticated enquire whether the red or green sauce is hotter and make their choice accordingly.

Blue Corn Crêpes

Yield: about 24 crêpes

These crêpes, rolled with preserves and sprinkled with powdered sugar, are delicious for breakfast. They freeze well, so it's worth making up all of the batter even if you're not planning to serve the whole batch at once. They will thaw nicely in a warm oven. Use two pans instead of one to speed up the cooking.

1 cup all-purpose flour
½ cup blue cornmeal
6 tablespoons sugar
Pinch of salt
3 eggs

4 tablespoons unsalted butter, melted
1¾ cups warm milk
2 drops vanilla extract
½ teaspoon tequila (optional)
Canola or vegetable oil

Mix the flour, cornmeal, sugar, and salt together in a mixing bowl. Break the eggs into the dry ingredients and mix together.

In another bowl, mix the melted butter, milk, vanilla, and tequila together. Gradually add the liquid mixture to the flour mixture, stirring constantly. When the ingredients are thoroughly incorporated, refrigerate the batter for at least 2 hours.

Lightly grease a nonstick 6- or 7-inch pan or heavy cast-iron skillet with the oil, and warm it over medium heat. Remove the pan from the heat and ladle in between 2 and 3 tablespoons of the batter. Quickly tilt the pan so that the batter coats the whole of the bottom of the pan paper thin. Return the pan to the heat and cook the crêpe for about 1¼ minutes, until the edges curl a little. Flip the crêpe over with a spatula or your fingertips and cook the other side for about 30 seconds. The first side should be lightly browned, the second speckled with brown dots. Remove and keep warm, but not hot, or the crêpes will dry out.

Repeat the process for the remaining batter, adding a little oil to the pan each time.

Crispy Waffles

Yield: 6 waffles

What better way to trap syrup and all manner of toppings than the honeycomb impress of the waffle iron? What more comforting way to expend a week's worth of calories and cholesterol? We should forever be grateful to the Scandinavians, who bequeathed us waffles. To appease our consciences and relieve our waistlines, we serve fruit rather than syrup.

$1^2/_3$ cups all-purpose flour
$2/_3$ cup plus 1 tablespoon soda water
$1/_4$ cup clarified butter

$1^2/_3$ cups heavy cream
$1/_2$ teaspoon salt
Powdered sugar, for dusting
Fresh berries or fruit, for topping

To prepare the batter, mix the flour, soda water, and clarified butter together in a mixing bowl. In a separate bowl, whip the cream to stiff peaks. Fold the whipped cream into the flour mixture and add the salt.

Heat a waffle iron until it is hot, and pour in batter. Cook for between 5 and 6 minutes, until the waffle is crisp and golden brown. Transfer the waffle to a rack to rest briefly and then sprinkle it with a little powdered sugar. Top with fresh berries or fruit, or syrup if you prefer. Eat immediately as waffles do not reheat well.

La Luna Azul
Yield: 1 cocktail

The blue curaçao makes for a striking adaptation of the Margarita. Curaçao is the only generic orange liqueur (others are proprietary brands), and it is made with bitter oranges grown on the Caribbean island of Curaçao, off the coast of Venezuela. Curaçao liqueur comes in various colors for decorative effect; blue is probably the best known. This is one cocktail you should try more than once in a blue moon.

$1^1/_2$ ounces (3 tablespoons) tequila
$3/_4$ ounce ($1^1/_2$ tablespoons) Cointreau liqueur
$1/_4$ cup fresh lime juice
1 tablespoon superfine sugar
$1/_2$ ounce (1 tablespoon) blue curaçao

In a cocktail shaker, combine all the ingredients and shake well. Serve in a Margarita glass over ice (the glass may be salt-rimmed if desired).

Breakfast Blini

Yield: 4 servings

Blini are Russian pancakes, traditionally made with buckwheat and served with smoked salmon or caviar. (They are sometimes made with baking powder, but are much better with yeast.) On the place de la Madeleine in Paris there is a marvelous establishment called Caviar Kaspia. Smoked salmon and caviar are the main products sold on the first floor and, in the restaurant above, the specialty of the house is probably the most decadent dish in the world not made with chocolate: several ounces of *malossol* caviar served on blini with melted butter poured around and a huge dollop of sour cream on top.

Here is La Casa Sena's version.

1 tablespoon active dried yeast
½ cup lukewarm water
¾ cup plus 1 tablespoon whole wheat flour
2 cups warm milk
3 eggs, separated
Salt to taste
Sugar to taste
1⅔ cups all-purpose flour

3 tablespoons clarified butter
3 tablespoons crème fraîche
Canola or vegetable oil
1 cup melted butter, sour cream, or crème fraîche
1 ounce American sturgeon caviar or other caviar of your choice
4 ounces smoked salmon

In a mixing bowl, dissolve the yeast in the water. Stir in the whole wheat flour and let the mixture stand for 10 minutes. Place 1 cup of the milk in a separate mixing bowl and add the egg yolks, reserving the whites. Add the salt and sugar, the yeast mixture, and the all-purpose flour, and let the batter rest for 2 hours.

Then add the remaining 1 cup milk, clarified butter, and *crème fraîche*. Whip the egg whites to stiff peaks and fold them in. Let the batter sit for another 30 minutes.

Heat 1 teaspoon of oil in a blini pan or cast-iron skillet over medium heat, and ladle enough mixture into the pan to form a 3- to 4-inch circle. Cook each side for between 2 and 3 minutes. Repeat with the rest of the batter, and serve the blini with the caviar and smoked salmon.

Blue Corn and Cheese Blintzes

Yield: 4 servings

Blintzes are not to be confused with blini, even if we do have the recipes follow each other. Blintzes are wafer-thin pancakes that are folded around a savory or sweet filling, and then fried and served with a topping. In this recipe, we use ricotta cheese, but you can fill the blintzes with fruit if you prefer. We had these on our breakfast menu for years because so many of our regular customers loved them. This recipe is for those customers, and for anyone else willing to try something a little different.

1 cup ricotta cheese
2 teaspoons vanilla extract
1 teaspoon milk
½ teaspoon sugar
Zest of ¼ lemon, julienned

8 tablespoons unsalted butter
8 Blue Corn Crêpes (page 15)
4 tablespoons strawberry preserves
4 tablespoons sour cream

To make the filling, thoroughly combine the ricotta cheese, vanilla, milk, sugar and lemon zest in a stainless steel bowl and set the mixture aside.

Melt 2 tablespoons of the butter in a skillet. Fill the crêpes using one-eighth of the ricotta mixture (about 1¼ tablespoons) and fry them in the skillet over medium heat for several minutes, until they are brown on both sides.

Warm the strawberry preserves in a saucepan. Serve each crêpe with 1 tablespoon warm preserves and top with 1 tablespoon sour cream, preferably piped out of a pastry bag.

Brunch Burritos

Yield: 4 servings

To the north of the state's largest city, Albuquerque, the locals pride themselves on "Northern New Mexico" cooking, a reference that may be difficult to distinguish from northern Mexican cuisine. In both places, recipes were developed more or less concurrently and by similar peoples: the Spanish and the rather disparate groups of native Indians. What differences there are may be attributed to the local availability of ingredients. The advent of Tex-Mex cooking has further blurred the lines of demarcation but, in general, you will find hotter chiles, more extensive use of blue corn, and different cheeses in the foods of northern New Mexico.

This is the classic brunch dish in Santa Fe and one that gives eggs and ham a wonderful Southwestern twist.

4 large Whole Wheat Tortillas (page 38), warmed
8 eggs, scrambled
2 cups Green Chile Sauce (page 160)

1¼ cups grated Monterey Jack cheese
1¼ cups grated Cheddar cheese
4 thin slices prosciutto

Preheat the broiler.

Place the tortillas on serving plates. On each tortilla place one-quarter of the scrambled eggs, 2 tablespoons chile sauce, 1 tablespoon of each cheese, and one slice of the prosciutto. Roll up the tortillas and top them with the remaining chile sauce and cheese.

Place under the broiler to melt the cheese and serve immediately.

Bailando Fresas

Yield : 1 cocktail

These "dancing strawberries" combine the intriguing fruit flavors of orangey triple sec, pineapple, lime, and of course, strawberries.

1½ ounces (3 tablespoons) tequila
1 ounce (2 tablespoons) triple sec liqueur
¼ cup sliced fresh or frozen strawberries
1 tablespoon pineapple juice
1 tablespoon fresh lime juice
1 ice cube

Place all the ingredients in a blender and mix until smooth. Pour the drink into a tall glass.

Roast Beef Burritos
with Hatch Green Chile

Yield: 4 servings

This is a simple, robust brunch dish ideal for using leftover roast beef. The New Mexico green chiles that we use in our sauce come from Hatch in the southern part of the state, where the warmer climate and soil conditions suit them so well. If the volume of the annual crop is anything to go by, Hatch may qualify as chile capital of the world. In nearby Las Cruces, the agriculture school of New Mexico State University specializes in the study of chiles. Dr. Paul Bosland, an associate professor of horticulture, is the pepper breeder there, and has built an amazing greenhouse containing chiles of every conceivable color, shape, size, and heat quotient.

4 large Whole Wheat Tortillas (page 38)
12 ounces (or 8 to 12 slices) thinly sliced roast beef
2 cups Green Chile Sauce (page 160)
2½ cups grated Cheddar cheese
1 cup Spanish Rice (page 169), for serving
2 cups Black Beans (page 168), for serving
Shredded lettuce, for garnish
4 cherry tomatoes, for garnish

Place the tortillas on serving plates. On the middle of each tortilla place 2 or 3 slices of the beef and cover with ½ cup green chile sauce and ¼ cup of the cheese. Roll up the tortillas and top them with the remaining chile sauce and cheese. Place the burritos under the broiler to melt the cheese.

Serve each burrito with ¼ cup Spanish rice and ½ cup black beans. Garnish with the lettuce and tomatoes.

Tequila Diablo
Yield: 1 cocktail

This tequila cocktail is really a punch drink served in a glass. Make sure you're sitting down when you try this, and plan not to drive anywhere.

¾ ounce (1½ tablespoons) tequila
½ ounce (1 tablespoon) dark rum
½ ounce (1 tablespoon) triple sec liqueur
½ ounce (1 tablespoon) gin
½ ounce (1 tablespoon) vodka
Juice of 1 lemon
Splash of cranberry juice
1 tablespoon superfine sugar
Splash of 7-Up

In a cocktail shaker, combine the tequila, rum, triple sec, gin, vodka, lemon juice, cranberry juice, and sugar. Shake well, pour the drink into a tall glass over ice, and add the 7-Up.

Vegetable Burritos
with Red Chile

Yield: 4 servings

If you don't eat meat or eggs, or just want a change, this is the brunch burrito for you. The Green Chile Sauce (page 160) may be substituted for the red, or use both, if you prefer. The word burrito means "little donkey" in Spanish, and it is a mystery how this dish got its name. Some say burritos were invented by an *hombre* who sold them from a cart pulled by a diminutive equine. . . . *¿Quién sabe?*

4 Whole Wheat Tortillas (page 38)
2 tablespoons olive oil
1 zucchini, halved lengthwise and thinly sliced
1 yellow squash, halved lengthwise and thinly sliced
1 red bell pepper, quartered, seeded, and thinly sliced

1 cup cherry tomatoes, halved
1½ cups Red Chile Sauce (page 159)
2½ cups grated Cheddar cheese
Salt and freshly ground black pepper to taste

Preheat the oven to 350°F. Keep the tortillas warm, wrapped in a towel, in an ovenproof dish.

Heat the oil in a large skillet and sauté the zucchini, squash, bell pepper, and tomatoes over medium heat for between 3 and 5 minutes. Place a portion of the sautéed vegetables in the middle of each tortilla. Pour 1 tablespoon of the chile sauce over the vegetables, and sprinkle 2 tablespoons of the cheese on top of the sauce.

Roll up each tortilla and turn it, seam-side down, on the dish. Pour the remaining chile sauce over the burritos and sprinkle the remaining cheese on top. Bake the burritos in the oven until the cheese has melted and started to brown.

Carne Adovada Enchiladas
with Green Chile

Yield: 4 servings

Carne adovada is another trademark of northern New Mexico cooking, and it should be a tongue-sizzler. It was created by the early settlers as a practical as well as delicious means of preserving fresh pork. The most fiery and flavorful red New Mexico chiles come from the northern part of the state, especially around Chimayó and Dixon. Perhaps this has to do with the cooler fall weather during the ripening season, or soil conditions that enhance the flavor of the mature red chiles. It is intriguing that red and green New Mexico chiles — one the ripe, the other the unripe (immature) form of the same variety of chile — grow best in different parts of the state and in different microclimates.

1 cup canola or vegetable oil
12 blue corn or yellow corn tortillas
2 cups Carne Adovada (recipe follows)
3¾ cups grated Cheddar cheese
1½ cups Green Chile Sauce (page 160)

Preheat the oven to 350°F.

Heat the oil in a skillet. Immerse the tortillas in the hot oil for 3 seconds per side to soften. Drain them on paper towels, place them in a large baking dish, and keep them warm.

Fill the tortillas with the carne adovada, half of the cheese, and half of the chile sauce. Roll up the tortillas, and return them, seam-side down, to the baking dish. Cover the tortillas with the remaining chile sauce and cheese. Bake in the oven until the cheese has melted and started to brown, about 5 to 10 minutes.

Carne Adovada   Yield: about 5 cups

2 tablespoons olive oil

1 pound pork, trimmed and diced into ¹/₂-inch cubes

4 cloves garlic, finely chopped

4 shallots or ¹/₂ onion, finely chopped

1 teaspoon ground cumin

1 teaspoon dried oregano

Salt and freshly ground black pepper to taste

4 cups chicken stock

2 cups Red Chile Sauce (page 159)

Heat the oil in a heavy-bottomed pan or skillet and sauté the pork over medium-high heat until it is lightly browned. Add the garlic, shallots, cumin, oregano, salt, and pepper, and cook for 5 minutes longer.

Add the chicken stock and chile sauce, bring to a boil, reduce the heat, and simmer the mixture gently, covered, for 1 hour. Continue to cook uncovered for another 30 minutes.

Palace Avenue in the '30s showing both Sena Plaza in the background and Prince Plaza in the foreground.

Catalina Enchiladas

Yield: 4 servings

The word enchilada literally means "in chile." No wonder when a visitor occasionally asks for the chile in an enchilada dish to be served on the side — or, horror of horrors, left out entirely — muffled expletives in the native Spanglish tongue of Santa Fe are heard emanating from the *cocina*.

1 cup canola or vegetable oil,
    for frying
12 blue corn or yellow corn
    tortillas
1½ pounds cheddar cheese,
    grated (7½ cups)
½ cup diced onion

3 cups Red Chile Sauce (page 159)
1 cup Spanish Rice (page 169),
    for serving
2 cups Posole (page 168),
    for serving
Shredded lettuce, for garnish
4 cherry tomatoes, for garnish

Heat the oil in a skillet. Immerse the tortillas in the hot oil for 3 seconds per side to soften. Drain on paper towels, place them in a large baking dish, and keep them warm.

Fill each tortilla with ⅓ cup of the cheese, 2 teaspoons onion, and 2 tablespoons chile sauce. Roll up the tortillas and return them, seam-side down, to the baking dish. Cover the tortillas with the remaining chile sauce and cheese. Place the enchiladas under the broiler to melt the cheese.

Serve each portion with ¼ cup Spanish rice and ½ cup *posole*. Garnish with the lettuce and tomatoes.

New Mexico Sangria
Yield : 8 to 12 servings

This is the archetypal wine cooler that originated in Spain. The fruit brandies are not absolutely necessary, but they give the recipe an extra dimension. Use a red Burgundy-type wine or even a red Spanish wine.

2 limes, cut into ½-inch-thick slices
2 lemons, cut into ½-inch-thick slices
2 oranges, cut into ½-inch-thick slices
2 maraschino cherries
1 bottle (750 ml) dry red wine
½ ounce (1 tablespoon) blackberry brandy
½ ounce (1 tablespoon) cherry brandy
½ ounce (1 tablespoon) apricot brandy
½ ounce (1 tablespoon) strawberry brandy
½ ounce (1 tablespoon) crème de cassis
½ ounce (1 tablespoon) Bonny Doon Framboise (raspberry wine), or puréed and sieved frozen raspberries
1½ cups fresh orange juice
¾ cup pineapple juice
1 liter bottle Sprite, 7-Up, or sparkling water

Gently crush the slices of fruit and place them in a large pitcher filled with ice. Add the remaining ingredients, except the Sprite or 7-Up, and stir well. Serve the sangria in tall glasses and top each cocktail with a generous splash of Sprite, 7-Up, or sparkling water for carbonation.

Turkey Enchiladas

Yield: 4 servings

Chicken enchiladas are a traditional staple of the Southwest. This adaptation, using turkey meat instead, is a great way to use up holiday-season leftovers in a creative way. If you're not afraid of the heat of the flavorful chile sauce, you'll find this Santa Fe-style enchilada far superior to those of other parts of the region.

1 cup vegetable oil, for frying
12 blue corn tortillas
5 cups grated Cheddar cheese
2 cups cooked diced turkey meat,
* preferably breast*

3 cups Green Chile Sauce
* (page 160)*
¾ cup sour cream
Chopped lettuce, for garnish
8 cherry tomatoes, for garnish

Heat the oil in a skillet and fry the tortillas one by one for 3 seconds on each side to soften them. Fill each tortilla with ¼ cup of the Cheddar cheese, 2½ tablespoons of the turkey, and 2 tablespoons of the green chile sauce. Roll up the tortillas and arrange 3 together snugly on each plate. (These plates should be heatproof.)

Combine the sour cream and the remaining green chile sauce and pour the mixture over the enchiladas, covering them completely. Sprinkle the remaining cheese over the top. Heat the enchiladas under the broiler until the cheese melts. Garnish with the lettuce and cherry tomatoes.

Huevos Rancheros

Yield: 4 servings

This is our adaptation of the classic Mexican dish of ranch-style eggs. The original version calls for a tomato-based *ranchero* sauce; in this recipe, the New Mexican red chile sauce gives it plenty of bite. The addition of *posole*, a quintessential New Mexican corn dish, contributes to the Southwestern credentials of this dish. Posole made from blue corn is, however, difficult to find in most places outside the region, so regular posole (hominy to y'all in Dixie) may be substituted, although it won't be quite the same. In any event, cook the posole as we suggest in the recipe on page 168.

½ cup vegetable oil
4 blue or yellow corn tortillas
1 cup blue corn posole (page 168)

2 cups Red Chile Sauce (page 159)
4 eggs
1¼ cups grated Cheddar cheese

Heat ¼ cup of the oil in a skillet. Immerse the tortillas in the hot oil for 3 seconds per side to soften. Drain them on paper towels and keep them warm. Place ¼ cup of the posole on each serving plate (use heatproof plates that can go under the broiler) and cover with a tortilla. Pour 2 tablespoons of the chile sauce on each tortilla to cover.

Heat the remaining vegetable oil in a skillet, fry the eggs, and place one on each serving plate, on top of the chile sauce and tortilla. Cover the eggs with the remaining sauce and top with the grated cheese. Place the plate under a broiler to melt the cheese.

Opposite page:
Breakfast Blini, page 17.

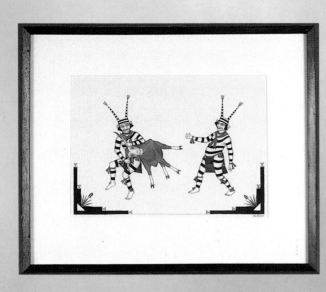

Two-Striped Flying Dance
Tsirah Awa

Single Figure – Hopi
Tuva Hoena

Watermelon
Harrison Begay

Sena Frittata

Yield: 4 servings

Strictly speaking, a *frittata* differs from an omelet in that, usually, the filling ingredients are mixed together with the eggs before they are cooked rather than being folded inside during the cooking process. Frittatas (which are Italian in origin) are also cooked over lower heat and are usually left unfolded. This recipe can be made that way, but we actually prepare it in the traditional omelet manner — we prefer the manner omelet but the name frittata. This dish may also be made with a red chile sauce, which is sometimes more easily obtained as it can be made from rehydrated dried red chiles.

12 eggs
4 tablespoons unsalted butter
2¹/₂ cups grated Cheddar cheese

1¹/₂ cups Green Chile Sauce
(page 160)

Whisk the eggs in a bowl. Melt 1 tablespoon of the butter in a heavy-bottomed pan or skillet over medium-high heat. When the butter begins to sizzle, pour one-quarter of the whisked eggs into the skillet and shake the pan vigorously until the eggs begin to set, about 1 to 2 minutes. Use a spatula or plastic scraper to scrape down the sides of the pan.

Sprinkle ¹/₃ cup of the cheese over the frittata, and fold it over. Cook for 1 minute longer, and transfer the frittata to a serving plate. Keep warm, and repeat the process for each of the remaining 3 frittatas.

Cover the frittatas with the chile sauce and sprinkle the remaining cheese on top. Place the dish under a broiler to melt the cheese.

Chocolate Tequila Colada

Yield : 1 cocktail

The Piña Colada ("strained pineapple") is a tropical-flavored cocktail which became very popular during the 1970s. In this version tequila replaces the rum and the addition of chocolate gives it a new spin.

1½ ounces (3 tablespoons) tequila

½ ounce (1 tablespoon) cream of coconut, such as Coco López brand

1 tablespoon fresh lime juice

1 tablespoon pineapple juice

1 tablespoon superfine sugar

3 tablespoons half-and-half

1 tablespoon chocolate chips

Place all the ingredients in a blender and mix until chocolate chips are smoothly incorporated. Pour the drink into a tall glass over ice.

Roasted Corn Omelet
with Goat Cheese and Wild Mushrooms

Yield: 4 servings

This recipe contains ingredients that are part of the long and rich culinary heritage enjoyed in Santa Fe. Wild mushrooms grow abundantly in the Sangre de Cristo and Jemez mountains on either side of The City Different. Corn has been grown for centuries by the Pueblo Indians of the Rio Grande valley and by their ancestors before that. Goats, brought to the Southwest by the Spanish settlers, were important livestock, used for their milk and cheese, meat, and skins.

12 eggs
1 teaspoon salt
½ cup clarified butter
6 ounces fresh wild mushrooms such as chanterelles, shiitakes, or button mushrooms, sliced

3 shallots, finely chopped
6 ounces fresh goat cheese, sliced
1½ cups roasted corn kernels, from 2 ears (see page 162)

Whisk the eggs and salt in a mixing bowl and set aside.

To make the filling, heat ¼ cup of the butter in a large skillet and sauté the mushrooms and shallots quickly over high heat. Mix in the cheese and add the corn. Remove the pan from the heat and set it aside.

To make each of the omelets, heat 1 tablespoon of the remaining butter in a heavy-bottomed pan or skillet over high heat until it is almost smoking. Pour one-quarter of the whisked eggs into the skillet and shake the pan vigorously until the eggs begin to set, about 1 to 2 minutes. Use a spatula or plastic scraper to scrape down the sides of the pan. Add one-quarter of the mushroom mixture to the center of the omelet, slide the omelet out of the pan onto a serving plate and, at the same time, fold it over.

Keep the omelet warm, and repeat the process for the remaining omelets.

Santa Fe Eggs Benedict

Yield: 4 servings

In this Southwestern version of Eggs Benedict, we use avocado in the Hollandaise sauce and, instead of English muffins, our own sage *bolillos*.

4 Sage Bolillos (page 42)
2 tablespoons unsalted butter
8 slices hot smoked ham
  or crisp bacon

8 poached eggs
1 cup Avocado Hollandaise
  (recipe follows)

Preheat the oven to 350°F.

Cut the bolillos in half, spread them with butter, place them on a cookie sheet, and toast them in the oven for 5 minutes.

Set two halves of the toasted bolillos on each serving plate, and place a slice of ham on each half. Place a poached egg on the ham and top with 2 tablespoons of the Avocado Hollandaise.

Avocado Hollandaise   Yield: about ¼ cup

½ cup (1 stick) unsalted butter
3 egg yolks
1 tablespoon lemon juice

½ avocado, mashed into a smooth
  purée

In a saucepan, melt the butter over low heat.

In a double boiler or over a water bath, beat the egg yolks for 1 minute. Add the lemon juice and continue to beat until the mixture starts to thicken, about 1 to 2 minutes longer.

Remove the eggs from the heat and whisk the melted butter into them gradually, in droplets at first. Continue whisking until the sauce thickens, ideally to the consistency of mayonnaise. (Be warned that it turns from liquid to thick very suddenly.) Fold in the avocado until well incorporated and use immediately.

Sena Gravlax

Yield: 10 to 12 brunch servings; 20 to 24 appetizers

It is always best to buy a whole salmon with the head still on because it is far easier then to judge its freshness. The eyes should be convex and shiny, not clouded, and the gills should have some bright red blood. Of course, "the nose always knows." The salmon should smell fresh and of the ocean. Unless you're handy with a sharp knife, have the fishmonger fillet the two sides of the salmon for the *gravlax*. Once filleted, the salmon will keep for a week to ten days in the refrigerator.

½ cup sugar
½ cup salt
3 tablespoons crushed peppercorns

1 whole salmon (about 6 to 8 pounds), boned and cut into 2 fillets with skin on
2 bunches fresh dill, coarsely chopped (about 1 cup)

In a mixing bowl, combine the sugar, salt, and peppercorns. Place the salmon fillets skin side down and side by side on a clean work surface. Rub the salt mixture into the fillets and sprinkle the dill over them.

Place one fillet on top of the other, head over tail. Lay out enough plastic wrap to cover the fillets 4 or 5 times. Carefully move the fillets over to the plastic and wrap them up tightly. Place the package in a rectangular pan that easily accommodates it. Place a 7- to 10-pound weight over the salmon fillets, making sure that it weighs down the salmon evenly and completely.

Transfer the pan to the refrigerator and let the fish marinate for 3 days, turning the package on the second day. After the third day, carefully remove the salmon from the marinade and slice the fillets thinly.

Serve gravlax with warm sliced red potatoes, capers, fresh dill, mustard, and warm toast.

Bloody Maria
Yield : 1 cocktail

This distinctly Southwestern version of the classic Bloody Mary can also be made with tequila. Garnish with a celery stalk or a slice of lime.

1½ ounces (3 tablespoons) vodka
¾ cup Maria Muerta mix (recipe follows)

Mix well and serve the drink over ice in a tall glass.

Maria Muerta Mix
Yield : About 4½ cups, enough for 5 cocktails

1 quart canned tomato juice
¼ cup pure red chile powder
2 teaspoons Worcestershire sauce
½ teaspoon Tabasco sauce
1 tablespoon freshly ground black pepper
1 tablespoon fresh lime juice

Thoroughly combine all the ingredients.

Red Chile Linguine and Rock Shrimp
with Cilantro Pesto

Yield: 4 servings

The red chile in the linguine heralds a melding of two great cuisines: Italian and Southwestern. The classic basil *pesto* takes on an interesting twist when it's made with cilantro, one of our most commonly used herbs. Not that pestos are that different from Mexican *pipiáns* that date from pre-Columbian times, and pine nuts (*piñones*) are native to New Mexico as well as to the Mediterranean.

Cilantro Pesto   Yield: about 2 cups

1 bunch cilantro

1 cup olive oil

2 cloves garlic

$^1\!/_2$ cup piñones (pine nuts)

$^1\!/_2$ cup grated Asiago cheese

1 pound Sandia Chile Pasta Dough (page123)

1 pound rock shrimp

$^1\!/_2$ cup white wine

1 bunch scallions, thinly sliced

To prepare the pesto, plunge the cilantro into a pan of boiling water, remove it immediately, and revive it in ice water. When cooled, cut off the stems and discard them. Transfer the cilantro to a blender and add the olive oil, garlic, nuts, and the cheese. Blend until the mixture is smooth.

Using a pasta machine, roll the pasta dough out into a sheet and let it dry for 10 minutes. Cut the sheet into 9- to 12-inch lengths and then cut each length into linguine. Cook the pasta in boiling water until *al dente*. Meanwhile, simmer the rock shrimp in the white wine for 2 minutes. Strain the pasta and the shrimp and place them in a mixing bowl. Toss with the pesto and scallions until evenly mixed.

Southwest Sena Burgers

Yield: 4 servings

Ah! The ubiquitous burger. The average American consumes three burgers a week, which translates to around 40 billion a year across the country. A question most of us face at one time or another is: How do we jazz them up? We like to think that this recipe, with the tortilla and green chile sauce, gives the classic American burger an appealing Southwestern twist.

1½ pounds ground round beef
Salt and freshly ground black
*   pepper to taste*
4 Whole Wheat Tortillas (page 38)
4 teaspoons Dijon mustard
4 teaspoons Mayonnaise
*   (page 161)*

½ cup Green Chile Sauce
*   (page 160)*
½ cup grated mozzarella cheese
2 tomatoes, thinly sliced,
*   for garnish*
1 red onion, thinly sliced,
*   for garnish*
½ head lettuce, for garnish

Prepare the grill.

Form the ground beef into 4 patties, each weighing about 6 ounces, and season them with salt and pepper. Grill the burgers to the desired doneness. Alternatively, they may be sautéed.

Set a tortilla on each serving plate, and place a hamburger in the middle of each tortilla. Spread 1 teaspoon each of the mustard and mayonnaise on top of the burger, and add 2 tablespoons of the green chile sauce. Top with 2 tablespoons of the grated cheese, and wrap up the tortillas, placing each one seam-side down on the plate. Garnish with the tomato and onion slices, and lettuce leaves (torn or shredded if desired).

Casa Club Sandwich

Yield: 4 servings

Any smoked turkey will do, but one smoked with mesquite will have the best flavor. At least mesquite is good for something, because it's the scourge of many a Southwestern rancher. The tree sends its roots out an incredible distance to steal water from anything else around, and kills off grazing pasture as a result. Vast areas of Texas and the Southwest were once rich grasslands, changed forever by the greedy mesquite.

Tillamook cheese and *capocollo* are wonderful products that are worth searching for to make an unforgettable club sandwich, but you can substitute more familiar Cheddar and ham and still enjoy a classic lunch.

1/4 cup Mayonnaise (page 161)
1 canned chipotle chile, chopped
12 slices whole wheat bread or
  Sourdough Rye Bread (page 46)
1 head green lettuce
8 slices Tillamook Cheddar cheese

12 slices mesquite-smoked
  turkey breast
2 large tomatoes, cut into 12
  thin slices
8 slices hot capocollo
  or smoked ham

Thoroughly combine the mayonnaise and *chipotle* chile, and spread about 1 tablespoon of the mixture on each of 8 slices of the bread.

For each sandwich, place some lettuce on top of a slice of the spread bread. Add 2 slices of cheese and 2 slices of turkey. Place another spread slice on top, and add some more lettuce, 3 slices of tomato, 2 slices of smoked ham, and 1 more slice of turkey. Place a plain slice of bread on top of that to top off the sandwich.

Cut the sandwich diagonally into 4 pieces, and secure each section with a toothpick. Serve with fresh fruit, coleslaw, or french fries.

Long Island Iced Tea

Yield : 1 cocktail

This potent mixed drink (called Texas Tea in the Lone Star State) may look like iced tea, but there the similarity ends.

½ ounce (1 tablespoon) gin
½ ounce (1 tablespoon) vodka
½ ounce (1 tablespoon) light rum
½ ounce (1 tablespoon) tequila
½ ounce (1 tablespoon) triple sec liqueur
1 teaspoon fresh lemon juice
Splash of cola

In a cocktail shaker, combine the gin, vodka, rum, tequila, triple sec, and lemon juice. Shake well and pour the drink into a tall zombie (or hurricane) over ice. Add the cola.

Grilled Chicken Sandwich
with Red Chile Jelly

Yield: 4 servings

There is nothing quite so satisfying as a great grilled chicken sandwich. The red chile jelly is certainly worth making, but if you are short of time, you can always use the commercially available, green jalapeño jelly. Use the bread and cheese of your choice — one of the advantages of this recipe is that you can change the ingredients every time you make it.

4 boneless chicken half breasts (about 4 to 6 ounces each)
Salt and freshly ground pepper to taste
4 Sage Bolillos (page 42) or 8 slices of bread
¼ cup olive oil or butter
½ cup Red Chile Jelly (page 159)

8 slices jalapeño-flavored Monterey Jack or Cheddar cheese
½ cup Green Chile Sauce (page 160)
2 tomatoes, thinly sliced, for garnish
1 red onion, thinly sliced, for garnish
½ head lettuce, for garnish

Prepare the grill and preheat the oven to 350°F.

Season the chicken breasts with salt and pepper and grill them between 3 and 5 minutes, until done; alternatively, they may be sautéed. Cut the *bolillos* in half, brush each slice with the olive oil or butter and toast them in the oven for between 3 and 5 minutes or until they are a light brown.

Place four bolillo halves on serving plates, and spread the red chile jelly on the remaining halves. Place the chicken breasts on the plain bolillo halves, add the cheese, and top with the chile sauce. Close the sandwich with the bolillo halves that have been spread with the jelly. Garnish with the tomato and onion slices, and lettuce leaves (torn or shredded if desired).

Breads

*B*read has been a staple of civilizations since prehistoric times. Prohibitionists may be interested (and dismayed) to know that the by-product of making bread in days gone by was beer. According to Reay Tannahill in her fascinating book *Food in History* (Stein and Day, 1973), the Neolithic homemaker sprouted grain to add to bread to make it more digestible; then the grain was soaked in water and the fermented liquid poured off and drunk. In tracing the history of grain, Tannahill notes that some civilizations began to prefer the by-product to the bread itself: "It appears that 40 percent of the Sumerian grain yield was used for beer production. An ordinary temple workman received a ration of about 1.75 Imperial or 2.2 American pints a day, and senior dignitaries five times as much. . . ." Now that's a lotta Bud!

Bread making has advanced to the point that the baker may choose to drink beer, but he will not necessarily make any. There is an art to baking loaves with a fine, crusty exterior and a beautifully textured, soft interior. A good baker has an inherent feel for the dough that cannot be described in a recipe. Nonetheless, the recipes here are written so that the results should be rewarding if the instructions are followed carefully.

The history of bread made with wheat in the Southwest is relatively short. Wheat is not native to the Americas, and was introduced to the continent by the Spanish in the sixteenth century. The native Americans of the region had, however, prepared breads for hundreds of years before that, using corn, nuts, and seeds that were ground into flour. A form of leavening agent was made from fermented dried potato and cornmeal. The crisp *piki* flatbread of the Hopis has a particularly interesting history: It has been made for centuries in huts used specifically for the purpose.

The recipes that follow are good examples of the multicultural heritage enjoyed by the modern-day inhabitants of the Southwest, with influences drawn from the native American, Spanish, Mexican, and Anglo or Northern European cuisines and cultures.

Winter scene, Plaza, San Francisco Street at Lincoln Avenue ca. 1925. Courtesy Museum of New Mexico.

Whole Wheat Tortillas

Yield: about 10 tortillas

La Casa Sena was proud to host a dinner by Stephen Pyles of Dallas during a symposium on Southwestern cuisine held in 1989 and attended by such nationally recognized chefs as Mark Miller, John Sedlar, Robert Del Grande, Rick Bayless, and Dean Fearing. This is Stephen's recipe for flour tortillas, which we recommend along with his excellent cookbook, *The New Texas Cuisine* (Doubleday, 1993), for its innovative Texan twist on Southwestern cuisine and which is included here with kind permission.

½ cup whole wheat flour, preferably stone ground
½ cup all-purpose flour
¾ teaspoon salt

¾ teaspoon baking powder
2 to 3 tablespoons vegetable shortening
½ cup warm water

Sift the flour, salt and baking powder together in a mixing bowl. Using a fork or your fingers, cut in the shortening and mix until it is evenly distributed and the mixture has the texture of coarse cornmeal.

Stir about 3 tablespoons of the water into the dry ingredients, using only enough to form a soft dough. Knead the dough for about 20 seconds and form it into a ball. Gradually add another 2 tablespoons of water while working the dough with your hands. Periodically dip your fingers into the remaining approximately 3 tablespoons of water and continue to knead the dough for between 3 and 5 minutes longer. The dough should be soft and wet, but not sticky.

Divide the dough into 10 equal pieces. Stretch each piece out and fold the sides in toward the middle to form a round ball, about 1 inch in diameter. Place the balls of dough on a cookie sheet and cover with plastic wrap. Let the dough rest for between 5 and 10 minutes.

Dip each ball in flour to coat it lightly. Using your thumbs, gently stretch each ball into a 2-inch circle. On a clean work surface, roll each piece of dough into as thin a circle as possible.

Heat a cast-iron skillet over medium-high heat to about 425°F (a drop of water should sizzle on the skillet). Carefully lift each circle and place in the skillet. Cook the tortilla for about 35 or 40 seconds, until bubbles appear on the surface. Flip the tortilla with a spatula and cook it for an additional 5 or 10 seconds on the other side. Stack the tortillas and wrap them in a towel or foil to keep them warm.

Blue Corn Muffins

Yield: 12 muffins

We get more requests for these muffins than for any other item on our menus. Many food magazines have also asked us for the recipe. These colorful muffins are quintessentially Southwestern, with the blue corn that is still grown by the Native Americans of the region and the green chile.

8 tablespoons unsalted butter
$^1/_2$ cup sugar
2 extra-large eggs
1 New Mexico or Anaheim green chile, roasted, peeled, seeded, and chopped (about $^1/_2$ cup)
$^1/_2$ cup fresh corn kernels (from 1 ear), steamed until just tender

$^1/_2$ cup grated Cheddar cheese
$^1/_2$ cup grated Monterey Jack cheese
$^1/_2$ cup all-purpose flour
$^3/_4$ cup blue cornmeal
1 teaspoon baking powder
$^1/_2$ teaspoon salt
$^3/_4$ cup milk

Preheat the oven to 375°F.

In the bowl of an electric mixer, cream together the butter and sugar. Add the eggs and chopped green chile. Add the corn, cheeses, flour, cornmeal, baking powder, salt, and milk, and mix just until blended.

Divide the muffin dough into 12 pieces and place them in a well-greased, 12-muffin pan. Bake in the oven for 35 to 40 minutes or until a cake tester comes out dry. Turn the muffins out onto a rack to cool.

Whole Wheat Sopaipillas

Yield: about 30 sopaipillas

Sopaipillas are believed to have originated in the Albuquerque area of New Mexico in the 1700s. They resemble puffed-up pillows and must be served warm. Traditionally, they are made with white flour, fried in very hot (450°F) lard, sprinkled with sugar or honey, and eaten for dessert. If there are any left over, they become an entrée the next day, filled with refried beans, meat, or almost anything else.

In today's New Mexican cuisine, sopaipillas are often served as a bread without the sugar or honey. The whole wheat flour is a healthful Casa Sena innovation and adds a pleasant dimension to the flavor. In this recipe, the sopaipillas are baked. If you prefer to fry them, we recommend you use canola oil for health reasons.

½ tablespoon active dried yeast
2 cups lukewarm water
2 cups whole wheat flour
2 cups unbleached flour

½ tablespoon salt
1 teaspoon sugar
2 tablespoons vegetable shortening

Preheat the oven to 500°F.

In a bowl, dissolve the yeast in ⅓ cup of the water. In a large mixing bowl, combine the flours, salt, and sugar, and cut in the shortening. Add the dissolved yeast and the remaining water in increments, and mix thoroughly to form a dough. Knead for 5 minutes, and let the dough rest in a warm place for 20 minutes in a bowl covered with a damp towel.

Punch down the risen dough, roll it out to a thickness of ⅛-inch or thinner if possible, and cut it into 3- or 4-inch squares. Place the squares on a lightly greased cookie sheet and bake them in the oven for 10 to 12 minutes, until the sopaipillas are puffed and brown.

The punched-down dough can be formed into loaves to make an interesting whole wheat bread. Bake the loaf in a 350°F oven for 25 to 30 minutes.

Soft Dinner Rolls

This is a straightforward recipe for multipurpose simple rolls. We use these rolls for dinner, but of course they can accompany lunches and snacks, or be used for sandwiches. Their plainness is an advantage when they accompany highly seasoned Southwestern foods or dishes with delicate, complex flavors.

1 tablespoon active dried yeast
1½ cups milk, scalded and cooled
*   to lukewarm*
6 cups all-purpose flour

¼ cup sugar
½ tablespoon salt
4 tablespoons unsalted butter,
*   melted*

In a bowl, dissolve the yeast in ¼ cup of the lukewarm milk. In the bowl of an electric mixer fitted with a dough hook, mix the flour, sugar, and salt, and add the butter and dissolved yeast. Add the remaining milk in ¼-cup increments, and mix thoroughly for about 10 minutes, starting out at low speed and rising to medium speed after about 4 minutes, to form a dough.

Transfer the dough to a greased mixing bowl, cover with a damp towel, and let it rise in a warm place for 1½ hours. Punch the dough down, turn it out onto a lightly floured surface, and knead it for 5 minutes. Return the dough to the bowl, cover with a damp towel, and let it rise again for 50 minutes to 1 hour. Punch it down, turn it out and knead it for another 5 minutes.

Divide the dough into 4 pieces, and let them rest for 15 minutes. Shape each piece into 4 or 5 rolls, and place them on a large cookie sheet. Cover the rolls with a damp towel and let them rise again in a warm place for 30 minutes. Meanwhile, preheat the oven to 425°F.

Place the rolls in the oven and bake them for between 15 and 18 minutes, until they are golden brown. Turn them out onto a rack to cool.

Sage Bolillos

Yield: 10 to 12 rolls

Bolillos are small, crusty Spanish rolls that are also common in Mexico. They usually come plain, but you can flavor them with different herbs such as thyme, oregano, or rosemary, or spices such as cumin or coriander.

These rolls make great sandwiches — see the recipe for Grilled Chicken Sandwich (page 34) — and are perfect for Eggs Benedict (page 29).

1 tablespoon active dried yeast
4 cups all-purpose flour
2 tablespoons sugar
¾ teaspoon salt
½ cup (4 ounces) vegetable shortening

1¼ cups water
2 teaspoons dried sage flakes
1 egg
1 tablespoon milk

Place the yeast, 2 cups of the flour, sugar, and salt in the bowl of an electric mixer fitted with a dough hook, and combine them. Place the shortening and water in a saucepan and heat gradually until the shortening melts. Let the mixture cool until it is lukewarm, and then add it to the bowl with the dry ingredients and mix together. Add the sage and, with the mixer running, the remaining 2 cups of flour in ½-cup increments until a soft, elastic dough forms; it should not be sticky.

Cover the dough with a damp towel, and let it rise in a warm place for about 2 hours, or until it doubles in volume. Punch the dough down, turn it out onto a lightly floured surface, and divide it into 10 to 12 equal pieces. Roll out into a baguette shape and pinch the ends into points.

Place the rolls on a cookie sheet lined with parchment paper and slash the tops of the rolls with a knife or razor blade. Cover the rolls with a damp towel and let them rise again for about 1 hour, until they have doubled in volume.

Preheat the oven to 375°F.

Beat the egg with the milk to make an egg wash and brush the rolls. Bake them in the oven for between 15 and 20 minutes, or until they are golden brown. Turn them out onto a rack to cool.

Opposite page:
Fresh breads are a wonderful ingredient in every dining experience at La Casa Sena.

Landscape
Willard Marsh

Hopi Snake Dance
Frank Applegate

Rain on Hopi Desert
Frank Applegate

Galletas

Yield: 4 loaves

Galleta is the name for a small Southwestern loaf of bread and at La Casa Sena, we use it as an edible bowl for Black Bean Soup (see page 72 and the illustration opposite page 74). It makes an attractive as well as tasty presentation. Alternatively, this can be used as an all-purpose bread or made into rolls.

2 tablespoons active dried yeast
1¾ cups lukewarm water
3⅓ cups unbleached all-purpose flour

1 teaspoon sugar
¾ teaspoon salt
2 tablespoons vegetable oil

In a bowl, dissolve the yeast in ¼ cup of the water. In the bowl of an electric mixer fitted with a dough hook, mix the flour, sugar, and salt, and add the oil and dissolved yeast. Add the remaining water in increments, and mix thoroughly for about 10 minutes, starting at low speed and rising to medium speed after about 4 minutes, to make a dough.

Divide the dough into 4 equal pieces. Form each piece into a ball and let rise in a warm place and covered with a damp cloth for 30 minutes. While the dough is rising preheat the oven to 375°F. Place the loaves on a greased and floured cookie sheet and bake them in the oven for 20 minutes, or until they are golden brown. Turn the galletas out onto a rack to cool.

Goat Cheese Bread

Yield: 1 loaf

Goat cheese (*chiva* in Spanish and *chèvre* in French) comes in a range of shapes and a variety of textures, from moist and crumbly to dry and quite firm. The moist and crumbly type works best in this recipe. The cheese gives a nice tangy flavor to the bread, but you can add other ingredients, such as chopped pecans, walnuts, chiles, or herbs, to provide additional flavor and texture.

2 cups all-purpose flour
1 cup water
½ cup goat cheese

2 teaspoons active dried yeast
2 teaspoons salt

Lightly grease a 4- by 8-inch bread tin. In the bowl of an electric mixer fitted with a dough hook, combine the flour, water, and goat cheese, and mix at low speed for 4 minutes. Cover the dough with a damp towel, and let it rest in a warm place for 15 minutes.

Add the yeast and mix for 4 minutes at medium speed. Add the salt and mix for 3 minutes longer at medium speed. Cover the dough again with a damp towel and let it rise for 30 minutes. Punch the dough down, turn it out onto a lightly floured surface, and knead it for 5 minutes. Form the dough into a cylinder and place it in the prepared bread tin. Cover the tin with a damp towel and let the dough rise in a warm place for between 45 minutes and 1 hour. Meanwhile, preheat the oven to 425°F.

When it has risen to the top of the tin, score the top of the dough lengthwise with a very sharp knife or razor blade and bake it in the oven for between 45 minutes and 1 hour, or until the bottom of the loaf sounds hollow when tapped. Turn the loaf out onto a rack to cool.

Pumpernickel Rye Bread

Yield: 1 loaf

Pumpernickel is a coarse-textured dark bread of German origin that usually has a slightly sour taste; sometimes it is made with a sourdough starter. Traditionally, pumpernickel contains rye flour, which is a dark and relatively dense low-gluten flour. Because of this, it must be mixed with other, high-gluten flour to result in a well-risen loaf.

²/₃ cup all-purpose flour
²/₃ cup pumpernickel flour
¹/₃ cup dark rye flour
1 teaspoon cocoa powder
1 teaspoon caraway seeds
1 pinch salt

1 tablespoon active dried yeast
1 cup plus 1 tablespoon water
3 tablespoons vinegar
*1 tablespoon canola or
    vegetable oil*

Lightly grease a 4- by 8-inch bread tin. In the bowl of an electric mixer fitted with a dough hook, combine the flours, cocoa, caraway seeds, salt, yeast, water, and vinegar. Mix at low speed for 2 minutes, and then at medium speed for 5 minutes. Add the oil, and mix for 2 minutes longer at medium speed. Cover the dough with a damp towel, and let it rise in a warm place for 45 minutes.

Punch the dough down, turn it out onto a lightly floured surface, and knead it for 5 minutes. Form the dough into a cylinder and place it in the prepared bread tin. Cover the tin with a damp towel and let the dough rise in a warm place for about 1 hour.

Meanwhile, preheat the oven to 425°F.

When it has risen to the top of the tin, score the top of the dough lengthwise with a very sharp knife or razor blade and bake it in the oven for about 45 minutes, or until the bottom of the loaf sounds hollow when tapped. Turn the loaf out onto a rack to cool.

Sourdough Rye Bread

Yield: 2 loaves

Sourdough bread is distinguished by its tangy, and yes, slightly sour, flavor imparted by a special sourdough "starter." Starters are a little like European aristocracy or the families descended from members of the Spanish nobility who settled in the Southwest: the longer their claimed ancestry, the more respected they are. One resident of Phoenix has an outstanding sourdough starter that he brought from the Black Forest in Germany; it is reputed to be three hundred years old.

The dough for this bread is best prepared the day before you bake it, so that it can rise overnight.

1 teaspoon honey	*1 cup rye flour*
1½ cups lukewarm water	*1 teaspoon salt*
1 cup Sourdough Starter	*½ teaspoon sugar*
(recipe follows)	*1 tablespoon caraway seeds*
3 cups all-purpose flour	

In the bowl of an electric mixer fitted with a dough hook, dissolve the honey in the water and then add the 1 cup starter. Add 2¼ cups of the all-purpose flour, mix thoroughly (the consistency will be lumpy), and let this "sponge" rest for 1 hour.

Add the remaining ¾ cup all-purpose flour to the sponge, together with the rye flour, salt, sugar, and caraway seeds. Mix for 2 minutes at low speed until the ingredients are thoroughly incorporated, and then for 6 minutes at medium speed. Transfer the dough to an oiled bowl, cover with a damp towel, and let it rise in a warm place overnight.

The next day, lightly grease two 4- by 8-inch bread tins. Punch the dough down, turn it out onto a lightly floured surface, and knead it for 5 minutes. Form the dough into two cylinders and place them in the prepared bread tins. Cover the tins with damp towels and let the dough rise in a warm place for between 3 and 4 hours.

Preheat the oven to 400°F. When they have risen to the top of the tins, score the tops of the loaves lengthwise with a very sharp knife or razor blade and bake them in the oven for about 45 minutes, or until the bottom of the loaves sound hollow when tapped. Turn the loaves out onto a rack to cool.

Sourdough Starter

The starter needs to be made well ahead of time; it can take up to a week before it is ready to use.

1 cup water
1½ cups rye flour
1 teaspoon salt

1 teaspoon sugar
1 medium potato, peeled
   and grated

In a mixing bowl, thoroughly combine all the ingredients and transfer them to a 2-quart glass jar fitted with a screw top. Leave off the screw top but cover the jar with cheesecloth and let rest in a warm place (about 80°F) for 24 hours.

Stir the starter and then cover the jar with plastic wrap. Let it rest for another 3 days in a warm place, stirring it every day. Then place the jar (with the top screwed on tightly) in the refrigerator. After 2 days, there should be a clear liquid on top of the starter, which indicates that it is ready to use.

Remove 1 to 2 cups at a time and replenish what you have taken with similar quantities of fresh ingredients. For example, if you are taking 1 cup of starter, replenish it with ½ cup rye flour and ½ cup water. If you are taking 2 cups of starter, replenish them with 1 cup of each. Leave the replenished starter at room temperature for 1 hour and then refrigerate.

Sourdough Olive Bread

Yield: 2 loaves

San Francisco became famous for its sourdough during the California gold rush of the mid-nineteenth century when yeast was hard to find. The city is still famous for its excellent sourdough bread, although some bakers cheat a little bit by using yeast for leavening and adding a commercial sour flavor.

This bread is a popular variation that we sometimes bake at La Casa Sena. One tip for success in creating a hard crust is to place a pan of water in the bottom of the oven.

1 tablespoon molasses
1¼ cups water
¼ cup milk
1 cup Sourdough Starter
* (see page 47)*

4½ cups all-purpose flour
½ teaspoon salt
¼ teaspoon sugar
½ cup sliced pitted black olives

In the bowl of an electric mixer fitted with a dough hook, dissolve the molasses in the water and milk and then add the 1 cup starter. Add 2¼ cups of the all-purpose flour, mix thoroughly (the consistency will be lumpy), and let this "sponge" rest for 1 hour.

Add the remaining flour to the sponge, together with the salt and sugar. Mix for 2 minutes at low speed until the ingredients are thoroughly incorporated, and then for 4 minutes at medium speed. Add the olives, and mix for another 2 minutes at medium speed. Transfer the dough to an oiled bowl, cover it with a damp towel, and let it rise in a warm place overnight.

The next day, lightly grease two 4- by 8-inch bread tins. Punch the dough down, turn it out onto a lightly floured surface, and knead it for 5 minutes. Form the dough into two cylinders and place them in the prepared bread tins. Cover the tins with damp towels and let the dough rise in a warm place for between 3 and 4 hours.

Preheat the oven to 400°F.

When they have risen to the top of the tins, score the tops of the loaves lengthwise with a very sharp knife or razor blade and bake them in the oven for about 45 minutes, or until the bottom of the loaves sound hollow when tapped. Turn the loaves out onto a rack to cool.

Appetizers

O f all the courses in a restaurant, appetizers are probably the most fun. The custom of "grazing" — sampling a number of appetizers and desserts without filling up with a main course — has become fashionable in recent years, and it does have the advantage of letting the diner taste a wide variety of dishes on a given menu.

You can tell a lot about a restaurant by the range and quality of the appetizers. At La Casa Sena, we take care to keep a wide variety of first courses on the menu. These change seasonally and sometimes more often just to keep our more frequent customers on their toes. Soups and salads are appetizers too, but they have their own chapters, so this one includes everything else. Most of our appetizers are Southwestern or have a strong regional twist.

Our extensive wine list has been assembled with appetizers as much in mind as main courses, and it can be delightfully challenging to match some of our wines with our first courses. Among the most frequently ordered white wines for our appetizers, and rightly so, are the grassy-toned Californian or French Sauvignon Blancs. Fruity, sweeter wines such as Gewürztraminer and Riesling go well with chiles because the wine and the chiles affect different parts of the palate.

Champagne is the perfect way to begin any meal, although its popularity has been somewhat tarnished by the advent of the inferior (and sometimes awful) imitations made by the bulk method. (Properly, the second fermentation takes place in the bottle.) The good sparkling wines, whether from France, California, or New Mexico, are well worth the difference in price.

Among the domestic sparkling wines, we recommend the Schramsberg which became famous when President Nixon served it at official functions during his historic trip to China. Domaine Chandon, made in California by the French producer, Moèt et Chandon, is one of our most popular wines. Surprisingly, New Mexico boasts an excellent sparkling wine of its own. A Blanc de Noirs, made by Gruet from pinot noir grapes grown near Elephant Butte in southern New Mexico, it has won many awards and is even exported to California.

Plaza. Courtesy Museum of New Mexico.

Red Onion Salsa

Yield: 4 servings; about 2 cups

This is the "house" salsa at La Casa Sena, and although we make it *picante*, as is the custom in northern New Mexico, it is easy enough to reduce the *chile caribe* if you prefer. We teach our waiters to count on their fingers when reciting the salsa recipe to our guests so that they don't miss any of the ten ingredients. We once hired an ex-cowboy who had lost a finger in a roping accident; he never did get the recipe right.

3 plum tomatoes (about 6 ounces), finely chopped
$1^{1}/_{2}$ red onions, minced
2 large cloves garlic, minced
$^{1}/_{4}$ cup fresh lime juice, with pulp
1 tablespoon chile caribe (dried red chile flakes)

3 tablespoons minced fresh parsley
$^{1}/_{2}$ tablespoon salt
$^{1}/_{2}$ tablespoon dried oregano
$^{1}/_{2}$ tablespoon ground cumin
2 tablespoons olive oil

In a glass or ceramic mixing bowl, thoroughly combine salsa ingredients. Serve with blue corn chips.

Guacamole

Yield: 4 servings; about $3^{1}/_{2}$ cups

The two main varieties of avocado are the Haas and Fuerte. We prefer the bumpy-skinned, purplish Haas for its firmer texture and more buttery, nuttier flavor. If you can only find unripened avocados, chivvy them along by placing them in a secured paper bag or by burying them in flour; they ripen quickly in the dark. Use guacamole as soon as you can as the green avocado flesh oxidizes and turns brown before too long.

4 ripe avocados, peeled, pitted, and coarsely chopped
1 clove garlic, finely chopped
1 jalapeño chile, finely chopped
1 teaspoon salt

1 tomato, finely chopped
Juice of 1 lime
$^{1}/_{4}$ onion, finely chopped
$^{1}/_{2}$ teaspoon pure red chile powder

In a large mixing bowl, combine all the ingredients. Serve with corn chips.

Cantina Nachos

Yield: 4 servings

In some restaurants, cheese *nachos* are known as Mexican pizza. In the Cantina, we make them with blue corn chips, which have become very popular of late. As well as having a distinctive flavor, they are high in nutrients. A Hopi from Arizona once told us that God gave the Hopi blue corn because it took much talent and hard work to grow; He gave white corn to the Navajo because it required some knowledge and some work; but He gave yellow corn to the white man because it grows all by itself.

1 large bag (10 ounces) blue corn chips
1½ cups Green Chile Sauce (page 160)

4 cups grated queso fresco, mozzarella, or Cheddar cheese (or a mixture)
3 Roma tomatoes (about 6 ounces), diced
1 cup pitted and diced black olives

Preheat the oven to 350°F.

Divide the chips between 4 ovenproof plates. Spoon the chile sauce over the chips and sprinkle the cheese on top. Bake in the oven until the cheese has melted, about 5 minutes.

Remove the plates from the oven and sprinkle the tomatoes and olives on top.

Sena Margarita
Yield : 1 cocktail

Margaritas are a mainstay in Santa Fe and by far the most popular cocktail. One of the reasons for La Casa Sena's preeminent reputation in the field is that we are constantly squeezing fresh lime juice. Yesterday's lime juice has already oxidized; only today's will do.

1½ ounces (3 tablespoons) gold tequila
1 ounce (2 tablespoons) triple sec liqueur
¼ cup freshly squeezed lime juice
1 tablespoon superfine sugar

In a cocktail shaker, combine all the ingredients and shake well. Serve in a Margarita glass over ice (the glass may be salt-rimmed if desired).

Corn Tamales

Yield: 8 tamales; 4 servings

Tamales are a traditional Mexican food, and every region of the country has its own style. The basic variety is invariably made with *masa* dough (a mixture of hominy-type corn, baking powder, and lard) wrapped in a softened dried corn husk to form a cylinder, and then steamed. In many parts of Mexico, the dough is flavored with local ingredients — herbs, meat, or vegetables; in the more tropical Yucatán region, for example, the dough is often wrapped in banana leaves. In New Mexico, tamales were originally a Christmas tradition, and the gathered family members would all pitch in to make them. Tamales are versatile and can be served as an appetizer or with a main course as a starch. Note that *masa harina* is a special form of ground corn; regular cornmeal is not a substitute.

10 large dried corn husks

Masa Dough

⅔ cup vegetable shortening,
*   at room temperature*
2 cups masa harina
¾ teaspoon salt

1 teaspoon baking powder
1 cup warm chicken stock or water
½ cup fresh corn kernels (1 small
*   ear), ground in a food processor*

Soak the corn husks in a large bowl of hot water for 20 to 30 minutes, until they are soft and pliable.

Meanwhile, prepare the masa dough. In the bowl of an electric mixer, whisk the shortening until it is light and fluffy, scraping down the sides with a spatula as necessary. In a separate bowl, mix the masa harina, salt, and baking powder. Gradually add the stock or water to make a dough, and then whisk the dough into the shortening. Mix in the ground corn kernels. The dough should be sticky, and have the consistency of cookie dough; add more liquid if necessary.

Drain the corn husks and pat them dry. Tear 2 of the husks into strips lengthwise, making 16 strips for tying the tamales. Divide the tamale dough evenly among the husks and spread it in the center, leaving 1 inch at each end of the husk uncovered. Roll up the husks to enclose the dough completely. Twist each end and tie with one of the torn-off strips.

Using a steamer, colander, or vegetable basket set over a saucepan of lightly boiling water, steam the tamales for between 40 and 45 minutes; the pan should be covered tightly. The tamales are cooked when the dough comes away easily from the husk.

Slit the cooked tamales lengthwise with a knife, and push the ends together slightly so it is easier to reach the contents (the husk should not be eaten). These tamales can be served plain, or with red or green chile sauce, if desired (pages 159 and 160).

A view of the enclosed courtyard in Sena Plaza ca. 1950.

Black Bean Tamales

Yield: 8 tamales; 4 servings

Tamales can be filled with a variety of ingredients — pork *carnitas*, smoked chicken, seafood, mushrooms, and even fruit and cinnamon for a sweet version. The possibilities are endless and they are as perfect for leftovers as for specially prepared fillings. This vegetarian tamale uses black beans, a Southwestern staple and traditional partner for corn.

10 large dried corn husks　　　　*1 recipe Masa Dough (page 54)*

Black Bean Filling

1 tablespoon canola oil　　　　　*2 cloves roasted garlic, minced*
1 shallot, minced　　　　　　　　　*(page 162)*
1 cup puréed cooked black beans　*2 teaspoons sherry vinegar*

Soak the corn husks in a large bowl of hot water for 20 to 30 minutes, until they are soft and pliable. Meanwhile, prepare the tamale dough.

To prepare the beans, follow the recipe on page 71 for Vegetarian Black Bean Soup, drain the cooked beans, measure out 1 cup and purée them, reserving the rest together with the liquid for soup or another use.

Heat the oil in a heavy skillet or cast-iron pan. Sauté the shallot over medium-high heat for 5 minutes until it is soft. Reduce the heat to medium, add the cooled and puréed black beans, roasted garlic, and vinegar, and sauté the mixture for between 10 and 15 minutes, until the beans begin to form a crust. Let the filling cool.

Drain the corn husks and pat them dry. Tear 2 of the husks into strips lengthwise, making 16 strips for tying the tamales. Divide the tamale dough evenly among the husks and spread it in the center, leaving 1 inch at each end of the husk uncovered. Divide the filling evenly on top of the dough, leaving a little space at each edge. Roll up the husks to enclose the dough and filling completely. Twist each end and tie with one of the torn off strips of corn husk.

Using a steamer, colander, or vegetable basket set over a saucepan of lightly boiling water, steam the tamales for between 40 and 45 minutes; the pan should be covered tightly. The tamales are cooked when the dough comes away easily from the husk.

Slit the cooked tamales lengthwise and push the ends together slightly so it is easier to reach the contents (the husk should not be eaten).

Shrimp and Smoked Cheddar Flautas

Yield: 4 servings

Flautas (Spanish for flutes) are tiny, deep-fried rolled appetizers, like little enchiladas. For a Southwestern variation on this recipe, you can make the pesto with cilantro rather than with the traditional basil.

Basil Pesto   Yield: About 2 cups

2 bunches fresh basil

1 cup sundried tomatoes

¹/₂ cup toasted piñones (pine nuts)

1 tablespoon minced garlic

¹/₂ cup olive oil

Salt and freshly ground pepper to taste

8 to 12 medium shrimp, peeled and deveined

¹/₂ red bell pepper, seeded and finely julienned

¹/₂ green bell pepper, seeded and finely julienned

1 yellow bell pepper, seeded and finely julienned

2 scallions, split and finely julienned

2¹/₂ cups grated smoked Cheddar cheese

4 Whole Wheat Tortillas (page 38)

Vegetable oil, for frying

To make the pesto, place all the ingredients in a blender or food processor and blend until they are finely minced.

Marinate the shrimp in the pesto for about 8 hours in the refridgerator. Transfer the shrimp and pesto to a sauté pan and cook over medium heat for 3 minutes until the shrimp are pink and cooked through. Cut each shrimp into 3 or 4 pieces and let them cool. Transfer the shrimp to a mixing bowl and combine with the bell peppers, scallions, and cheese.

Divide the filling among the tortillas, roll them up, and secure them lengthwise with a toothpick. Fill a large skillet with oil to a depth of 1 inch and heat the oil to 325°F. Deep-fry the flautas for between 3 and 5 minutes over medium-high heat until they are golden brown. Remove the toothpicks, cut the flautas in half, and serve them with any salsa.

Muy Margarita
Yield : 1 cocktail

This version uses a premium brand of aged, 100 percent blue agave tequila and lemon juice, which is less tart than the more usual lime juice.

1 ounce (2 tablespoons) El Tesoro añejo tequila

1 ounce (2 tablespoons) Cointreau liqueur

Juice of ¹/₂ a lemon

Juice of ¹/₂ a lime

1 tablespoon superfine sugar

In a cocktail shaker, combine all the ingredients and shake well. Serve in a Margarita glass over ice (the glass may be salt-rimmed if desired).

Marinated Shrimp Quesadillas

Yield: 4 servings

A good way of thinking about *quesadillas* is as the Mexican or Southwestern equivalents of sandwiches. They are highly versatile because you can fill them with almost any kind of meat, or seafood such as shrimp, as well as vegetables, together with a good melting cheese. Quesadillas are also an excellent way of using up leftovers.

*1 recipe Epazote Marinade for
   Shrimp (page 165)*
*8 ounces small shrimp (about 15
   to 20), peeled and deveined*
1 tablespoon olive oil

8 Whole Wheat Tortillas (page 38)
*2¹/₂ cups grated Asiago or
   Monterey Jack cheese*

Preheat the oven to 350°F.

Combine the ingredients for the marinade in a glass or ceramic mixing bowl and marinate the shrimp for 30 minutes.

Heat the tablespoon of olive oil in a sauté pan or skillet. Drain the shrimp, reserving the marinade. Sauté the shrimp over medium-high heat for about 2 minutes, until they are pink and cooked through. Add 2 to 3 tablespoons of the reserved marinade, combine with the shrimp, and remove from the heat.

Evenly divide the shrimp among four tortillas, spreading the mixture to cover each tortilla. Sprinkle the grated cheese over the shrimp, and place the remaining four tortillas over the shrimp and cheese mixture.

Place the quesadillas on a large cookie sheet and cook them in the oven for between 5 and 6 minutes, until the cheese melts. Alternatively, the quesadillas may be cooked in a sauté pan over medium-high heat, or broiled until the cheese melts. Remove the quesadillas and cut each one into 4 or 6 equal slices.

*Opposite page:
Blue Corn Fried Oysters
with Habenero Salsa,
page 60.*

Eight Dancers
Qwa Pi

The Fast
Wa-ka

Hopi Ceremonial Dance
Mootska

Chile Rellenos
with Chiva Cheese, Corn, and Pine Nuts

Yield: 4 servings

At La Casa Sena this dish is often served as a main course for lunch, but it makes a great appetizer, especially if you use small *poblano* chiles. Poblanos, commonly used in Mexico, are relatively mild, at least in their green (unripe) state. The piquancy in this dish is provided by the red chile sauce, but the heat is partially offset by the goat cheese. All dairy products have a moderating effect on the heat of chiles, and milk and yogurt are particularly effective antidotes.

¾ cup fresh corn kernels (1 ear)
½ cup toasted piñones (pine nuts)
½ cup golden raisins
4 ounces fresh goat cheese (chiva)

4 poblano chiles, stems intact, roasted, and peeled
1 cup grated Cheddar or Monterey Jack cheese or a mixture of both
1 cup Red Chile Sauce (page 159)

Preheat the oven to 350°F.

Mix the corn, pine nuts, raisins, and goat cheese together in a mixing bowl. Make a lengthwise slit in each chile, carefully remove the seeds, and stuff them with the mixture. Place the stuffed chiles on a baking sheet, top with the grated cheese, and bake in the oven for 20 minutes.

Place ¼ cup of the chile sauce on each serving plate. Remove the *rellenos* from the oven and serve them on top of the sauce.

Blue Corn Fried Oysters
with Habanero Salsa

Yield: 4 servings

Oysters tend to be at their best in the fall and winter; during the summer they reproduce and are often less tasty and more flabby. Oysters have long been considered an aphrodisiac and, as it turns out, there may be some scientific basis for this claim. They are a great source of zinc, and studies have shown that zinc deficiency is connected to a lack of libido and delayed adolescence in children.

Habanero Salsa   Yield: 1 cup

1 fresh habanero chile, seeded and minced

1 cup Red Onion Salsa (page 52)

1 quart vegetable oil, for deep-frying

20 fresh oysters, shucked
½ cup blue cornmeal

To prepare the salsa, blend the *habanero* and the red onion salsa until smooth.

Heat the oil in a deep fryer to 350°F.

Coat the oysters in the cornmeal and deep-fry them for 3 to 4 minutes or until they are golden brown.

Serve 5 oysters per plate, with the salsa on the side.

Kir
Yield : 1 cocktail

Father Kir was the heroic mayor of Dijon in France during World War II. He enjoyed adding a little black currant liqueur to his glass of white wine and, because of his reputation as a resistance fighter (and because the combination works well), this cocktail was named after him. This recipe works best with a dry white wine such as a crisp Sauvignon Blanc. It's important to remember that this drink is only as good as the quality of the ingredients you use.

½ ounce (1 tablespoon) crème de cassis (black currant liqueur)
6 ounces (¾ cup) chilled dry white wine

Pour the crème de cassis into a balloon-shaped wine glass and then pour in the wine.

Grilled Shiitake Mushrooms
with Chipotle Dijonnaise Sauce

Yield: 6 servings

Shiitake mushrooms are native to Japan and the Far East, but they are now being grown in many parts of the United States. A few years ago, an educational program brought growing techniques to the Navajo, so don't be surprised if you find the delicacies attributed to these native Americans. Shiitakes bring a good price but they are very labor intensive; the spores must be seeded in wet oak logs and the growing process is lengthy. Their peak season is the summer and fall.

Chipotle Dijonnaise Sauce
Yield: about ⅞ cup

1 large egg yolk, at room temperature
½ cup extra virgin olive oil
2 tablespoons white wine vinegar

1 tablespoon Dijon mustard
2 chipotle chiles en adobo, puréed
1 to 2 tablespoons Sauvignon Blanc wine

18 large fresh shiitake mushrooms, washed and stems removed
1 tablespoon vegetable oil

½ cup Parmesan cheese, freshly grated
1 small bunch chives, finely chopped

To make the sauce, whisk the egg yolk with an electric mixer until it is thick and light in color. With the mixer still running, slowly drizzle in some of the olive oil and whisk until the mixture starts to thicken. Add a few drops of the vinegar, whisk them in, and continue alternating gradual additions of the oil and vinegar until the mixture is thick and well blended. Fold in the mustard and chipotle purée, and add enough wine to make a thick, pourable sauce.

Lightly brush the mushrooms with the vegetable oil. Grill them for 4 or 5 minutes per side, or until they begin to soften.

Pour the sauce onto serving plates and place 3 grilled mushrooms on each plate. Sprinkle the cheese and chives over the mushrooms.

Kir Royale
Yield : 1 cocktail

For this adaptation of the traditional recipe, use one of the excellent American sparkling wines made by the méthode champenoise, which is distinguished as such on the label. Of course, an imported French champagne will do just fine, but avoid using a cheap, bulk-processed sparkling wine.

½ ounce (1 tablespoon) crème de cassis (black currant liqueur)
5 ounces (½ cup plus 2 tablespoons) champagne or domestic sparkling wine

Pour the crème de cassis into a champagne flute, and then pour in the champagne or sparkling wine.

Mini Pizzas
with Wild Boar Sausage and Manchego Cheese

Yield: 4 servings

Manchego is the most famous of Spanish cheeses and originates in the plain of La Mancha. (No doubt the rain in Spain that falls mainly on the plain contributes to the lush grass diet of the sheep that produce the firm, salty, and somewhat piquant cheese.) Wild boar (*javalina*) is raised on ranches in Texas, and with its slightly gamey flavor makes great bacon, sausages, and ham that fit right in to the Southwestern repertoire.

Pizza Dough

$2^{1}/_{2}$ *teaspoons active dried yeast*
$^{1}/_{2}$ *cup lukewarm water*
2 cups all-purpose flour
$^{3}/_{4}$ *cup rye flour*

1 teaspoon salt
$^{1}/_{4}$ *cup milk*
3 tablespoons olive oil

Topping

2 scallions, finely sliced
2 jalapeño chiles, seeded
  and chopped
1 pint cherry tomatoes, halved

8 ounces wild boar sausage
  or pepperoni, sliced
$2^{1}/_{2}$ *cups grated Manchego cheese*
  or mozzarella

To make the dough, dissolve the yeast in the lukewarm water.

In a large mixing bowl, combine the flours and salt. Add the dissolved yeast mixture, and the milk and oil in increments, and mix thoroughly to form a dough. Knead the dough for 5 minutes, and let it rest in a warm place for 1 hour in a bowl covered with a damp towel.

Place a large baking sheet in the oven. Preheat it and the oven to 425°F.

Turn out the dough onto a clean, floured surface, and divide it into 4 equal pieces. Roll each piece out into a thin ($^{1}/_{8}$-inch thick) circle, about 6 inches across. Place the circles of dough onto the preheated baking sheet and sprinkle the scallions and *jalapeños* onto the dough. Then add the tomato halves, sausage or pepperoni, and finally the cheese. Bake the pizzas in the oven for between 10 and 15 minutes, until the dough has browned and the cheese has melted.

Mini Pizzas
with Dungeness Crab

Yield: 4 servings

Dungeness crab comes from the West Coast — it is caught as far north as Alaska. If it is unavailable, the Atlantic or Gulf blue crab will taste just as good. You can use a couple of *serrano* chiles instead of the *jalapeños*, but they should be seeded unless you enjoy really *picante* food. (The truly masochistic may want to substitute the fiery *habanero* — half a chile should be plenty.) Here's a useful kitchen tip: You'll find it easier to grate mozzarella cheese when it's frozen.

1 recipe Pizza Dough (see page 62)

Topping

2 avocados, peeled and pitted
Juice of ½ lemon
1 jalapeño chile, seeded and chopped

12 asparagus shoots, steamed and sliced
1 pound Dungeness crabmeat
2½ cups grated mozzarella cheese

Prepare the pizza dough and set it aside to rest for an hour.

Then, place a large baking sheet in the oven and preheat it and the oven to 425°F.

Turn the dough out onto a clean, floured surface, and divide it into 4 equal pieces. Roll each piece out into a thin (⅛-inch thick) circle, about 6 inches across.

Place the avocados, lemon juice, and jalapeño in a blender and purée the mixture.

Place the pizza dough circles onto the preheated baking sheet and spread the puréed avocado over them. Add the asparagus and crabmeat, and sprinkle the mozzarella on top. Bake the pizzas in the oven for between 10 and 15 minutes, until the dough has browned and the cheese has melted.

Almond Joy à la Mode
Yield : 1 cocktail

"Almond Joy's got nuts," the saying goes, which is where the hazelnut-flavored Frangelico liqueur comes in. Crème de cacao is a chocolate liqueur that is sometimes flavored with vanilla. This is a decadent cocktail worthy of any self-respecting chocolate lover.

¾ ounce (1½ tablespoons) Frangelico liqueur
¾ ounce (1½ tablespoons) white crème de cacao liqueur
¼ cup plus 1 teaspoon chocolate chips
Splash of cream of coconut, such as Coco López brand
2 tablespoons heavy cream
1 cup crushed ice

Place the liqueurs, ¼ cup of the chocolate chips, cream of coconut, cream, and ice in a blender. Blend, serve in a balloon glass, and garnish with the remaining teaspoon of the chocolate chips.

Venison Adovada Ravioli
with Chiva Crema and Salsa Verde

Yield: 4 servings

Wild venison tastes of the open range and the wild sage, juniper, and prairie grasses on which the deer graze. Some, however, prefer the less "gamey," grain-fed, farm-raised venison which has only recently become plentiful and which usually has more tender meat. In either case, venison is lean and delicious, and destined to become increasingly popular in the years to come.

Venison Adovada

2 tablespoons unsalted butter
2 tablespoons all-purpose flour
1/2 cup pure chile powder
1 tablespoon chile caribe (dried red chile flakes)

1 red jalapeño chile, seeded and minced
1/2 clove garlic, minced
2 cups water
6 ounces ground venison
Salt to taste

Chiva Crema   Yield: about 2 cups

2 cups heavy cream
1/2 teaspoon chopped garlic
1 tablespoon chopped basil
1/2 tablespoon chopped sage
2 scallions, white parts only, chopped

1/2 cup white wine
4 ounces (1/2 cup) fresh goat cheese, cut into slices
Salt and freshly ground pepper to taste

Salsa Verde   Yield: about 1 1/2 cups

1/2 cucumber, peeled, seeded, and chopped
1/2 bunch scallions, green parts only, chopped
3 tomatillos, husked, rinsed, and chopped
2 tablespoons white grapes, chopped

1/2 bunch cilantro, chopped
Juice of 1/2 lime
2 tablespoons unsalted butter
1/4 cup dry white wine
Salt and freshly ground pepper to taste

Ravioli

2 cups unbleached all-purpose flour

3 large eggs

To prepare the venison *adovada*, make a roux by melting the butter in a saucepan and stirring in the flour until the mixture is smooth. Add the chile powder, *chile caribe*, *jalapeño*, and garlic, and stir in the water a little at a time to make a sauce. Add the venison and braise until the meat is tender, about 8 to 10 minutes. Set aside to cool.

To prepare the *crema*, place the cream, garlic, herbs, scallions, and wine in a pan, and reduce the mixture by half. This will take about 10 to 15 minutes. Stir in the goat cheese thoroughly, and season with salt and pepper.

For the salsa, place the cucumber, scallions, tomatillos, grapes, cilantro, lime juice, butter, and wine in a large pan and cook over medium heat for 5 minutes. Season with salt and pepper. Keep chilled.

To prepare the ravioli, mound the flour onto a work surface and make a well in the center. Lightly beat the eggs in a bowl and pour them into the well made in the flour. Drawing some of the flour over the eggs, mix it in a little at a time until the dough is homogenous. Knead for 8 minutes.

Using a pasta machine or a rolling pin, roll out the dough to a thickness of $1/16$-inch. Cut the dough into long strips about 7 inches wide. Set 1 tablespoon-sized mounds of the venison adovada at 3-inch intervals down one side of each sheet of the pasta, setting the mounds about $1/2$ inch in from the edge. Carefully fold the other half of the pasta sheet over the mounds and press the edges firmly together. Using a pastry wheel, cut the mounds apart to make ravioli squares about 3 inches to a side. Trim the edges with the pastry wheel.

Bring a saucepan of water to a gentle boil and cook the ravioli until al dente. Remove and drain. To serve arrange 3 ravioli on each plate over a pool of the crema and spoon some of the salsa over the top in the center.

Sena Daiquiri
Yield : 1 cocktail

The original Daiquiri was created in Cuba at a restaurant called La Florida in Havana in the early part of this century. Purists differ on whether lemon or lime juice should be used to make the classic daiquiri and, in the absence of Cuban rum, on whether rum from Barbados, Jamaica, or Puerto Rico should be used.

$1\frac{1}{2}$ ounces (3 tablespoons) Myers' dark rum
Juice of 1 lemon
2 tablespoons superfine sugar

In a cocktail shaker, combine all the ingredients and shake well. Serve the drink in a brandy snifter over ice.

Tortillas de Papas

Yield: 6 servings

The word *tortilla* does not necessarily mean a form of flat bread; it is also a type of Spanish omelet. In Spain, this appetizer, much like a potato pancake, is usually served at room temperature. At La Casa Sena, we serve them hot. Either way, they're delicious.

1 teaspoon olive oil
1 tablespoon unsalted butter
4 large potatoes, peeled and thinly sliced
1 onion, thinly sliced

2 eggs
1 teaspoon cold water
Salt to taste
Cayenne powder to taste

Heat the oil and butter in a skillet and sauté the potatoes and onion over medium heat until they are brown and tender, about 15 minutes. Set the skillet aside briefly.

Meanwhile, in a mixing bowl, beat the eggs with the water and season with salt and cayenne. Pour the eggs over the cooked potatoes and onions and stir until the mixture begins to set and turn brown. Turn the tortilla over and brown it on the other side. Remove the tortilla from the heat, let it cool a little, and cut it into squares.

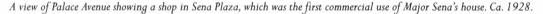

A view of Palace Avenue showing a shop in Sena Plaza, which was the first commercial use of Major Sena's house. Ca. 1928.

Fried Prickly Pear Cactus

Yield: 4 to 6 servings

This recipe is not just a novelty; cactus makes good eating. The Southwestern prickly pear or nopal cactus has flat, spiny, paddle-like leaves or pads. They are available at farmers' markets and some supermarkets in the Southwest, and at specialty produce stores elsewhere. These cactus leaves are usually sold with the spines removed. If they are not, you will have to do it yourself, armed with a knife or some pliers, protected by a pair of thick leather gloves.

2 large prickly pear cactus leaves (nopales)
3 eggs
1 cup milk
Pinch of salt
3 cups bread crumbs

1 teaspoon minced garlic
¼ cup minced cilantro
2 tablespoons pure chile powder
Canola oil, for deep-frying

Wearing thick gloves, remove the cactus spines if necessary by scraping them off with a knife or by pulling them out with pliers. Trim the edges and cut the leaves into strips ¼-inch wide.

In a bowl, beat the eggs together with the milk and salt to make an egg wash. On a large plate, combine the bread crumbs, garlic, cilantro, and chile powder.

Heat the canola oil in a deep-fryer to 375°F.

Dip the cactus strips into the egg wash, and then dredge them in the bread crumb mixture to coat them thoroughly. Deep-fry the strips for several minutes, until they are golden brown.

Drain on paper towels and serve with the salsa of your choice.

Singing Nun
Yield : 1 cocktail

This cocktail will give you that tropical feeling wherever you happen to be, and whatever time of year it is.

¾ ounce (1½ tablespoons) Myers' dark rum
¾ ounce (1½ tablespoons) Bacardi light rum
¾ ounce (1½ tablespoons) apricot brandy
2 tablespoons fresh lime juice
2 tablespoons fresh orange juice
2 tablespoons fresh pineapple juice
Splash of grenadine syrup

In a cocktail shaker, combine all the ingredients and shake well. Strain the mixture and serve the drink in a tall zombie (or hurricane) glass.

Vegetable Spring Rolls

Yield: 4 servings

Many Southwestern restaurants have experimented in adapting Oriental ingredients and recipes to the regional cuisine. This recipe is a prime example of a popular marriage of cultures.

You can substitute smoked dried *jalapeños* (*chipotle* chiles) for the fresh jalapeños. Chipotles are available in cans *en adobo* (in a vinegar sauce) from Southwestern, Mexican, and specialty stores. They can also be bought dried, in which case they should be rehydrated (see page 163) first.

4 spring roll wrappers	*1 red bell pepper, seeded and diced*
1 egg, beaten	*2 jalapeño chiles, seeded*
1 zucchini, diced	*and minced*
1 leek, thinly sliced	*2 teaspoons minced fresh ginger*
1 yellow bell pepper, seeded and diced	

Dipping Sauce   Yield: about ¼ cup

1 tablespoon white wine vinegar	*1 jalapeño chile, seeded and finely diced*
3 tablespoons olive oil	

Preheat the oven to 425°F.

Using half of the beaten egg, brush one side of each spring roll wrapper. Combine the vegetables and place one-fourth of the mixture in the center of the brushed side of each wrapper. Roll up the wrappers to form spring rolls. Brush the outside of the rolls with the remaining beaten egg. Bake the rolls in the oven for 10 to 15 minutes, until they are crisp.

Meanwhile, prepare the dipping sauce. Whisk together the vinegar and oil, and stir in the jalapeño. Serve the spring rolls with the sauce.

Mai Tai
Yield : 1 cocktail

This cocktail was created by Victor Bergeron, who founded Trader Vic's in California. Legend has it that Tahitian friends who tasted the prototype exclaimed mai tai — "out of this world!" Orgeat is a nonalcoholic syrup, made with almonds and sugar, that has a distinct almond flavor.

1½ ounces (3 tablespoons) dark rum

½ ounce (1 tablespoon) triple sec liqueur

½ ounce (1 tablespoon) orgeat

2 tablespoons superfine sugar

1 teaspoon fresh lemon juice

In a cocktail shaker, combine all the ingredients. Shake well and pour the drink into a cocktail glass over ice.

Soups & Stews

Soups and stews such as black bean soup and green chile stew are found on almost all authentic Santa Fe menus and vary in heat from the *picante* to the incendiary. Occasionally visitors have to be put out with foam. We have some fiery examples in this chapter, as well as some that do not actually include chile.

Another staple in Santa Fe is *menudo*, which is a traditional favorite for New Years Day. In fact, it is required eating if you are to have a good year, and it is also a popular hangover cure. Suffice to say that the smell and taste of the tripe that is the essential ingredient of menudo is, perhaps, sufficiently esoteric for we iconoclasts to omit the recipe.

La Casa Sena, like most restaurants, always has a soup *du jour* or in our case, a *sopa del día*. The soup of the day is clearly listed on our menus, which makes things easy for the waiter. Before a daily printing was practical, a room-service waiter at the Mayfair Hotel that I ran in St. Louis was heard to describe the item as "a very fine soup with just a little *du jour* in it."

Vegetarian Black Bean Soup

Yield: 8 servings

Of the two recipes for black bean soup offered in this chapter, this is the vegetarian version. Santa Fe is considered by many to be the Alternative Cure or Complementary Medicine capital of the nation, and it will come as no surprise that so many people here are vegetarians. There are also many here who believe in the curative powers of crystals. Although our puppy did recover miraculously from distemper when a friend tied a "specially programmed" crystal to its collar, I still suspect that, on a cold winter's day, there's no better alternative cure to the blues than this soup.

*4 cups dried black beans, rinsed
   and drained*
2 quarts water
2 sticks celery, sliced
2 carrots, sliced
2 onions, chopped
2 cloves garlic, chopped
2 bay leaves

2 cloves
Pinch of nutmeg
Pinch of cayenne powder
1 teaspoon mustard
1 tablespoon Worcestershire sauce
1 cup dry sherry
Salt to taste
8 lemon slices, for garnish

Place the beans and water in a large saucepan and bring them to a boil. Remove the pan from the heat and let the beans stand for 1 hour.

Add the vegetables, bay leaves, spices, mustard, and Worcestershire sauce. Return the pan to a boil, reduce the heat, and simmer the mixture for about 3 hours, until the beans are tender. Let the mixture cool and then purée it.

Return the soup to a clean saucepan, reheat it, and add the sherry and salt. Serve in soup bowls and garnish with the lemon slices.

Black Bean Soup en Galleta
with Tomato Salsa

Yield: 6 to 8 servings

This is our other version of black bean soup, which can also be enjoyed by vegetarians if the bacon is omitted. Served in a *galleta* loaf, it makes a striking presentation. Instead of croutons floating on top of the soup, the soup is sitting inside a giant crouton.

4 ounces bacon (optional)
¾ cup chopped celery
¾ cup chopped carrot
¾ cup chopped onion
2 garlic cloves, chopped
1½ tablespoons ground cumin
½ tablespoon dried oregano
½ tablespoon dried thyme
1 bay leaf
½ teaspoon cayenne powder

¼ cup tomato paste
8 ounces black turtle beans,
*   soaked overnight and drained*
6 to 8 cups vegetable
*   or chicken stock*
¼ cup fresh lime juice
½ bunch fresh cilantro, chopped
6 to 8 Galleta loaves (page 43)
Tomato Salsa (recipe follows)

In a large pan, cook the bacon until crisp. Add the celery, carrot, onion, garlic, cumin, oregano, thyme and bay leaf, cayenne, and tomato paste. Add the beans and stock, and simmer, covered, for about 2½ hours. Add more stock or water if needed. Transfer to a food processor or blender and purée. Just before serving, add the lime juice and cilantro.

Cut the tops off the galleta loaves and set them aside. Scoop out all the bread inside leaving a "wall" ½-inch thick. Press in the "wall" down toward the crust to form a more impervious shell. Ladle the soup into the loaves and garnish with tomato salsa, if desired.

Tomato Salsa   Yield: about 3 cups

½ cup chopped white onion
2 cups diced tomatoes
1 or 2 chopped jalapeño chiles

¼ cup chopped fresh cilantro
2 tablespoons fresh lime juice

In a glass or ceramic bowl, combine all the ingredients thoroughly.

This is a versatile salsa: It can be served finely or coursely chopped, or blended. It makes a wonderful accompaniment for chips.

Chilled Poblano Velouté

Yield: 6 to 8 servings

Velouté is a stock-based white sauce that is often used to make other sauces. Here it is used in an interesting and delicious soup. When we wrote the nation's first low cholesterol cookbook, *Eat to Your Heart's Content*, in 1972, we certainly couldn't have predicted that we would later publish any recipe using whipped cream as well as half-and-half. In defense, the co-author of that book, Kay "Cricket" Heiss, a registered dietician, notes that "not everyone has a cholesterol problem."

3 medium fresh poblano chiles
1 cup warm chicken stock
1 cup Gewürztraminer wine
1 teaspoon salt
2 cups half-and-half

2 cups heavy cream, whipped until frothy
Cilantro leaves, for garnish
Chiva croutons (recipe follows)

Roast the chiles under a broiler or on a grill, turning them frequently, until the skins are well blistered. Transfer them immediately to a paper bag and twist to secure. Let the chiles stand for 10 minutes. Peel the skins from the chiles, and remove the stem and seeds.

Transfer the chiles to a blender and purée them with the chicken stock and wine. Chill the mixture in the refrigerator. When chilled, stir in the salt, half-and-half, and whipped cream.

Serve the soup chilled in bowls, and garnish with cilantro leaves and chiva croutons.

Chiva Croutons   Yield: 4 cups

4 slices Sourdough Rye Bread (page 46)

4 ounces fresh chiva (goat) cheese

Lightly toast the bread slices under the broiler. Let them cool, spread them with the goat cheese, and lightly toast them again under the broiler. Remove the bread and cut it into croutons.

Sopa Verde

Yield: 8 servings

This soup can be made with practically anything edible that's green. So, if you have some beet or turnip tops or some Swiss chard in the refrigerator, throw them in the pot. And while we're on the subject, here's a piece of trivia: Which food do horses like best? Answer: Swiss chard. (Maybe they'd like this soup, too.)

8 cups chicken stock
4 ounces (2¾ cups) chopped
   fresh spinach
½ cup chopped, seeded, and peeled
   New Mexico green chile
½ green bell pepper, minced
¼ cup minced celery
¼ cup minced onion

½ cup diced zucchini
1 tablespoon chopped fresh basil
½ tablespoon dried tarragon
½ tablespoon dried sage
Salt to taste
1 avocado, peeled, pitted,
   and diced, for garnish

In a large pan, bring the chicken stock to a boil and add all the remaining ingredients except the avocado. Cook the soup over low heat for about 1 hour, stirring occasionally.

   Ladle the soup into bowls and sprinkle the avocado over the top before serving it.

Opposite page:
Black Bean Soup
en Galleta, page 72.

Silver Sky
Gustave Baumann

Singing Woods
Gustave Baumann

Spring Serenade
Gustave Baumann

Santa Fe Vegetable Soup

Yield: 8 servings

You can make this soup mild if you live in Olney, Illinois, or spicy hot for Tesuque, New Mexico, by adding more or less chile sauce. If you prefer, you can also purée the soup before adding the garnishes.

2 tablespoons unsalted butter
2 medium carrots, thinly sliced
2 sticks celery, diced
1 red bell pepper, cut into small triangles
1 green bell pepper, cut into small triangles
1 large onion, diced
1 teaspoon dried oregano
1 tablespoon chopped fresh basil
1 teaspoon ground celery seed
1 teaspoon coarsely ground pepper

8 cups chicken stock
1½ cups fresh corn kernels (from 2 ears)
½ cup cooked Posole (page 168)
¼ cup Red Chile Sauce (page 159)
¼ cup Green Chile Sauce (page 160)
Salt to taste
1 ounce blue corn chips, crumbled (about ½ cup), for garnish
1 avocado, peeled, pitted, and diced, for garnish

Heat the butter in a large pan and sauté the carrots, celery, peppers, and onion in it until they are soft. Stir in the herbs, celery seed, and pepper. Add the chicken stock, corn, *posole*, and the chile sauces. Bring the mixture to a boil, reduce the heat, and simmer for 10 minutes. Season the soup with salt and serve it in bowls, garnished with the corn chips and diced avocado.

Roasted Corn and Chipotle Soup

Yield: 4 to 6 servings

You can vary the heat of this soup by increasing or decreasing the quantity of *chipotle* chiles. If the chipotles are hard to find, you can rehydrate and purée the dried chiles (see page 163). If you have a small home smoker, you can even make your own from fresh *jalapeños*.

The marriage of the roasted corn and smoky chiles is one of the classic Southwestern flavor combinations, redolent of outdoor, campfire cooking that has long been practiced in the region.

*2 cups fresh corn kernels
    (from 3 ears)*
1 tablespoon vegetable oil
1 tablespoon unsalted butter
1 cup chopped onion
2 cloves garlic, minced
*1 can (28 ounces) tomatoes,
    drained and puréed*

2 teaspoons salt
*1/2 teaspoon freshly ground
    white pepper*
3 cups chicken stock
*2 canned chipotle chiles in adobo
    sauce, or to taste*

Preheat the oven to 400°F.

Place the corn in a single layer on a baking sheet and roast it for about 10 minutes, until it is browned.

Heat the oil and butter in a large pan and sauté the onion and garlic over medium-high heat until they are browned. Add the tomatoes, salt, pepper, and stock, and simmer for 5 minutes. Add the roasted corn and chipotle chiles, and simmer for 5 minutes longer.

Gazpacho

Yield: 6 to 8 servings

Gazpacho is a traditional Spanish soup from Andalusia. Served cold, it is the most refreshing food during the hot summer. For special occasions, we serve the soup in a hollowed-out extra-large beefsteak tomato. (Place the tomato on a bed of shaved ice before pouring the soup.) Another nice touch is to serve the soup with a small side bowl of garnish — a mixture of diced avocado, chopped scallions, garlic croutons, *chile caribe* (dried red chile flakes), and minced *jalapeños*.

¾ bunch celery
1 cucumber, peeled and sliced lengthwise
3 carrots
1 tablespoon chopped fresh basil
1 tablespoon chopped fresh dill leaves
1 tablespoon chopped fresh mint
½ tablespoon dried oregano
½ tablespoon dried tarragon
½ tablespoon freshly cracked black pepper
½ tablespoon minced garlic

½ tablespoon salt
½ tablespoon sugar
½ cup fresh lime juice
1 small red bell pepper, finely diced
1 small green pepper, finely diced
1 small onion, finely diced
1 tablespoon finely chopped parsley
4 cups tomato juice
2 cups crushed ice
Worcestershire sauce to taste

Mince the celery, cucumber, and carrots in a food processor or meat grinder and place them in a large mixing bowl. Add the herbs, pepper, garlic, salt, sugar, lime juice, bell peppers, onion, and parsley. Stir in the tomato juice and ice. Season to taste with Worcestershire sauce and additional salt. Serve chilled.

Tomato Garlic Soup

Yield: 4 to 6 servings

When garlic cloves are roasted or sautéed properly, they are remarkably mild and odorless. A cup of this soup might have enough garlic cloves floating in it to scare off any prom-bound teenager, but one taste and you'll agree it's delicious. At least the garlic will ward off all but the most evil of spirits.

3 tablespoons olive oil
15 cloves garlic, peeled
6 tomatoes, peeled, quartered, and seeded
6 cups light vegetable or chicken stock
½ tablespoon paprika
½ teaspoon cayenne pepper (or to taste)

Salt and freshly ground pepper to taste
2 ounces (about 1 cup) uncooked penne pasta
¼ cup grated Parmesan cheese
3 tablespoons chopped fresh parsley

Heat the olive oil in a saucepan with a thick bottom and sauté the garlic for 2 minutes; be careful not to let it brown. Add the tomatoes, stock, paprika, and cayenne, bring the mixture to a boil, and simmer it for between 1 and 1½ hours. Cook the pasta in boiling water until *al dente*.

Season the soup with salt and pepper and add the cooked pasta. Then add the Parmesan, and parsley.

Potato Leek Soup

Yield: 6 to 8 servings

One does wonder what the Irish ate before the native Americans discovered Columbus wandering around on a beach looking for the spice islands of the East. It's constantly amazing to contemplate the world without the products that Europeans brought back from the New World: potatoes, tomatoes, corn, chiles, and . . . tobacco. The best book on the subject of the foods of the Americas is *Indian Givers: How the Indians of the Americas Transformed the World* by J. McIver Weatherford (Crown, 1988).

3 tablespoons unsalted butter

1 yellow onion, chopped

4 leeks, white part only, cut in half and sliced

4 baking potatoes, peeled and cut into ¼-inch cubes

2 quarts light chicken or vegetable stock

2 tablespoons chopped fresh thyme (or 1 tablespoon dried thyme)

Salt and freshly ground white pepper to taste

2 tablespoons chopped fresh parsley

½ cup Croutons (page 162)

Heat the butter in a saucepan with a thick bottom and sauté the onion, leeks, and potatoes for 2 minutes. Add the stock, thyme, salt, and pepper. Bring the mixture to a boil and simmer it for between 40 and 50 minutes.

Transfer the soup to a blender and purée it. Serve with the parsley and croutons.

Carrot Soup

Yield: 4 to 6 servings

One thing you can be sure of is that a soup containing carrots and fresh orange juice is bound to be healthy. If you're afraid of all that goodness, what with the beta carotene and vitamin C, just add a dollop of sour cream on top.

3 tablespoons olive oil
1 yellow onion, sliced
2 pounds (7 or 8) carrots, peeled and sliced
Cayenne powder to taste
Salt and freshly ground pepper to taste

6 cups light chicken or vegetable stock
2 tomatoes, chopped
1 cup fresh orange juice
2 tablespoons chopped fresh parsley (optional)
2 tablespoons chopped crisp-fried bacon (optional)

Heat the olive oil in a saucepan with a heavy bottom and sauté the onion for 2 minutes. Add the carrots, cayenne, salt, and pepper. Add the stock, tomatoes, and orange juice, bring the mixture to a boil, and simmer it for between 30 and 40 minutes.

Transfer soup to a blender and purée it. Garnish with parsley and bacon, if desired.

Yellow Split Pea Soup

Yield: 4 to 6 servings

Split peas, also known as field peas, are grown specifically for drying. When dried, they split along a natural seam, hence their name. They come in different colors: yellow, green, and pink or red, so you might pick the color you want to use in this soup to match the dining room decor or your china pattern. We like the yellow ones.

4 ounces bacon, chopped

4 leeks, white part only, finely diced

1 carrot, peeled and finely diced

2 cups yellow split peas, soaked overnight and drained

6 cups light vegetable or chicken stock

1 tablespoon chopped fresh rosemary

1 tablespoon chopped fresh thyme

Salt and freshly ground pepper to taste

1 to 2 teaspoons Dijon or prepared mustard (optional)

2 tablespoons chopped fresh parsley, for garnish

In a saucepan with a heavy bottom, sauté the bacon for 2 or 3 minutes over medium high heat until it is browned. Drain most of the rendered bacon fat from the pan and add the leeks and carrot. (The bacon can be omitted and the vegetables cooked in a little olive oil.) Sauté the vegetables for 2 or 3 minutes.

Add the split peas and the stock, bring the mixture to a boil, and skim it. Add the rosemary and thyme and simmer the soup for between 1 and 1½ hours, or until the peas are soft. Season with salt and pepper, stir in the mustard if desired, and garnish with parsley.

Mushroom Sherry Soup

Yield: 8 servings

You can use domestic mushrooms, button mushrooms, or splurge with *shiitakes*, *chanterelles*, *cèpes*, or whichever wild mushrooms are available. It all comes down to personal taste and the size of your pocket book.

2 tablespoons unsalted butter	1/4 cup all-purpose flour
1 onion, chopped	8 cups warm chicken stock
2 sticks celery, chopped	2 cloves garlic, minced
1/2 medium leek, white part only, chopped	1 shallot, minced
3/4 teaspoon dried oregano	4 cups sliced mushrooms
1 1/2 teaspoons chopped fresh basil	1 tablespoon brandy
1/3 teaspoon dried rosemary	1/4 cup sherry
1/3 teaspoon dried sage	3/4 teaspoon salt
3/4 teaspoon ground celery seed	3/4 teaspoon coarsely ground black pepper

Melt 1 tablespoon of the butter in a saucepan and sauté the onion, celery, leek, herbs, and ground celery seed for 3 or 4 minutes until the vegetables are soft; be careful not to let them brown. Sprinkle on the flour, mix it in, and add the chicken stock, stirring well to dissolve the flour.

Meanwhile, melt the remaining tablespoon of butter in a skillet and sauté the garlic, shallot, and mushrooms for 3 or 4 minutes. Add the brandy and sherry, and, using a long match, carefully light the mixture, shaking the pan until the flames have died down. Add the mushrooms to the vegetable mixture and season with salt and pepper.

Sopa de Albóndigas

Yield: 8 servings

Sopa de albóndigas is a classic Mexican soup made from either chicken or beef, with meatballs or dumplings and vegetables. This is our Southwesternized version.

2 tablespoons unsalted butter
$^1\!/_2$ onion, chopped
$^1\!/_2$ bunch broccoli
$^1\!/_2$ cauliflower
2 carrots, sliced
$^3\!/_4$ jícama (about $1^1\!/_2$ cups), chopped
$^1\!/_8$ head green cabbage, chopped
1 zucchini, chopped
1 yellow squash, chopped
$^1\!/_4$ red bell pepper, seeded and chopped

2 cups Green Chile Sauce (page 160)
1 cup Red Chile Sauce (page 159)
1 tablespoon tomato sauce
2 quarts water
1 teaspoon dried oregano
1 tablespoon chopped fresh basil
$^3\!/_4$ teaspoon dried tarragon
$^3\!/_4$ cup vegetable oil
$^1\!/_2$ cup all-purpose flour

Meatballs

$^1\!/_4$ cup Red Onion Salsa (page 52)
4 ounces ground beef

4 ounces ground pork
1 egg

In a large saucepan, melt the butter and sauté the onion, broccoli, cauliflower, carrots, jícama, cabbage, zucchini, squash and red pepper until they are translucent. Add the chile sauces and the tomato sauce, and the water. Add the herbs and bring to a boil. Reduce the heat and simmer the mixture for 20 minutes.

Using a separate pan, make a roux by combing the oil and flour. Cook them over low heat until the floury taste is gone, about 5 minutes.

To make the meatballs, preheat the oven to 350°F. Combine the salsa, beef, pork, and egg, and roll the mixture into 1-inch balls. Place the meatballs on a baking sheet lined with parchment paper, and bake them in the oven for about 20 minutes.

Add the roux to the soup and stir until the soup has thickened. Add the meatballs just before serving.

Spiced Bosc Pear and Pepper-Jack Soup

Yield: 8 servings

The Spanish developed the winter Bosc pears (they are available from October through April or May) and brought them to the New World. The Spanish planted orchards of soft fruit in the Rio Grande valley and many are still producing fruit centuries later.

7 Bosc pears, peeled, seeded, and diced
2 quarts (8 cups) chicken stock
1/2 tablespoon honey
Pinch of pure chile powder
Pinch of nutmeg
Pinch of cinnamon

Salt and freshly ground white pepper to taste
1 cup heavy cream
1/2 cup grated pepper-flavored Monterey Jack cheese, for garnish
1/2 cup crumbled crisp bacon, for garnish

In a saucepan, combine the pears, stock, honey, chile powder, nutmeg, cinnamon, salt, and pepper. Bring the mixture to a boil, reduce the heat, and simmer for 4 or 5 minutes, until the pears are soft. Transfer the mixture to a food processor or blender and purée until smooth. Blend in the cream.

Serve the soup in bowls sprinkled with the grated cheese and bacon.

A view of the tea room that was built in 1930 where the stables had been. This area is now part of La Casa Sena.

Pueblo Lamb Stew

Yield: 10 to 12 servings

If you're lucky enough to get invited to eat at someone's house at one of the Indian pueblos in the Rio Grande valley, and it's a feast day when marvelous dances are held, the chances are good that you'll be served a wonderful lamb stew and the traditional *sopa* for dessert. We sometimes serve this stew at our sister Santa Fe restaurant, Blue Corn.

5 pounds lamb stewing meat, cut into 2-inch cubes

4 ounces pancetta or unsmoked ham

½ cup olive oil

1 teaspoon sugar

3 tablespoons all-purpose flour

Salt and freshly ground pepper to taste

2 cups lamb stock, veal stock, vegetable stock, or water

1 cup dry white wine

1 cup sliced carrots

1 cup sliced shallots

¼ cup chopped garlic

1 pound (about 8) Roma tomatoes, chopped

Chopped mixed fresh herbs, such as rosemary, thyme, parsley, and mint, for garnish

In a large pan, brown the lamb and pancetta in ¼ cup of the oil over high heat for 7 or 8 minutes. Sprinkle on the sugar and flour, toss the meat for about 4 or 5 minutes to cook evenly, and season with salt and pepper. Add the stock and wine, and simmer slowly, covered, for 1 hour.

Heat the remaining ¼ cup oil in a saucepan with a heavy bottom and sauté the carrots, shallots, garlic and tomatoes for 2 or 3 minutes. Add the vegetables to the lamb, and cook for 1 hour longer.

Sprinkle each serving with the mixed herbs and serve with boiled or roasted potatoes.

New Mexico Green Chile Stew

Yield: 4 servings

This straightforward dish is a classic that dates back centuries to the days of the earliest Spanish settlers in the region. Most of those settlers arrived from Mexico with their livestock — pigs, sheep, and goats — and stews using the indigenous chiles and vegetables were a staple of their diets. Green chile stew is a common denominator in most traditional New Mexican restaurants, and usually it's a good yardstick for judging the quality of the rest of the menu. For an authentic Southwestern touch, serve this dish with Blue Corn Muffins (page 39).

2 tablespoons canola oil

2 pounds pork butt (or any cut), trimmed and cut into $^1/_2$-inch dice

1 onion, diced

3 cloves garlic, finely diced

6 Roma tomatoes, diced

4 cups Green Chile Sauce (page 160)

2 teaspoons chopped fresh oregano

1 tablespoon chopped fresh cilantro

1 teaspoon ground cumin

Salt and freshly ground black pepper to taste

Heat the oil in a large saucepan and brown the pork for 4 or 5 minutes over medium-high heat. Add the onion and garlic and sauté for 2 or 3 minutes longer. Add the remaining ingredients and let the stew simmer, covered, for 1 to 1½ hours, or until the meat is tender. Add water if necessary (the pork should be at least two-thirds covered with liquid while it is cooking).

Salads & Dressings

*N*owhere are salads more important than they are in the United States, and Southwestern salads offer a welcome counterpoint to the often robust, *picante* flavors that characterize the cuisine. We are fortunate in Santa Fe in having a number of excellent organic growers, as well as others, who provide a constant supply and variety of first-rate lettuces, greens, tomatoes, and other produce. Of course, the availability of local ingredients is limited in winter, when our climate can be quite harsh in short spells, but with California and Texas so close, we are still able to serve the freshest, high-quality salad greens.

The popularity of salads in general owes much to the sizable segment of the population that is on a diet at any given moment. Many people, however, forget that the accompanying dressing often contains substantial amounts of oil. Although many are of the opinion that salads without a flavorful dressing are dull and lifeless, it's probably better to enjoy a salad for its flavor, texture, and nutritional value than for its questionable slimming qualities.

Most people like their salads quite cold and in some restaurants even the salad forks are chilled to enhance the effect of cool refreshing greens. On the flip side of that coin, the editor of our 1972 cookbook, *Eat To Your Heart's Content* noted that salads should be served at room temperature so as to maximize the flavors of the delicate ingredients. As with wines, and as the French say, *chacun à son goût.*

Sena Salad
with Artichoke Hearts, Jícama, and Local Feta

Yield: 4 servings

Jícama is a very distinctive, crisp and crunchy vegetable, and it has become increasingly available around the country. Try to buy smaller jícama that are heavy for their size. The feta cheese rounds out this salad nicely. If you can, always buy local feta, which will usually be the freshest.

Red-leaf lettuce
Bibb lettuce
2 large tomatoes, cut into 16 wedges
1½ cups jícama, peeled and julienned
8 canned or frozen artichoke hearts

8 thinly sliced red onion rings
¾ cup crumbled feta cheese
½ cup Guacamole (page 52)
16 blue corn chips
About ¾ cup House Dressing (recipe follows)

To assemble the salad, place the red-leaf lettuce on serving plates and the Bibb lettuce on top in the center of each plate. Arrange 4 tomato wedges, one-quarter of the jícama, and 2 artichoke hearts around the edge of the Bibb lettuce on each plate. Place 2 onion rings on top of the Bibb lettuce, and crumble the feta cheese over. Serve the guacamole on top of the lettuce and stick 4 of the chips into the guacamole on each plate.

Sprinkle 2 or 3 tablespoons of the dressing over each salad, avoiding the guacamole and chips.

House Dressing   *Yield: about 2½ cups*

2 ounces (1 can) anchovy filets
1 clove garlic
2 tablespoons fresh lemon juice

1 teaspoon freshly ground black pepper
½ cup red wine vinegar
1⅓ cups olive oil

Place the anchovies, garlic, lemon juice, pepper, and vinegar in a blender and purée. Transfer the mixture to a bowl and whisk in the oil until the ingredients are thoroughly combined. Stored in an airtight jar, it will keep for at least 2 weeks in the refrigerator.

Southwestern Caesar Salad

Yield: 4 servings

Traditionally, the egg in Caesar salads is raw. In this Southwestern version, it is parboiled to minimize (if not eliminate) the presence of any *salmonella* bacteria and it may be omitted entirely, if you prefer.

4 slices bread, ¹/₂-inch thick
   (preferably day-old bread)
1 head Romaine lettuce

Caesar Salad Dressing
   (recipe follows)

Preheat the oven to 350°F.

   To make the croutons, cut the bread into ¹/₂-inch cubes, toss them in about ¹/₄ cup of the dressing, and toast them in the oven on a cookie sheet for between 3 and 5 minutes until they are golden brown.

   To make the salad, discard the tougher outer leaves of the Romaine lettuce, separate the tender inner leaves, and place them in a large mixing bowl. Toss the lettuce with the remaining dressing, add the croutons, and divide the salad among 4 serving plates.

Caesar Salad Dressing   Yield: about 1¹/₂ cups

6 anchovy fillets
¹/₂ cup olive oil
¹/₂ cup grated Parmesan cheese
1 teaspoon freshly ground
   black pepper
1 egg

1 tablespoon white wine vinegar
1 tablespoon dry mustard
2 cloves garlic, peeled
3 tablespoons fresh lemon juice
Tabasco sauce to taste
Worcestershire sauce to taste

Place the anchovies, olive oil, Parmesan cheese, and pepper in a blender and blend for 1 minute. Boil the egg for 1¹/₂ minutes, peel it, chop it, and add it to the anchovy mixture. Add the vinegar, mustard, garlic, lemon juice, and Tabasco and Worcestershire sauces, and blend for 1 minute longer.

Opposite page:
Arugula Salad,
page 91, and below,
O'Keeffe Salad,
page 92.

Untitled
Ben Quintana

Single Kachina Figure
Loma Yesva

Eleven Dancers
Tonita Pena

Sun Symbol, Two White Dancers, Rainbow
Tse Ye Mu

Four Figures
Tse Yema

Squaw Dance
Harrison Begay

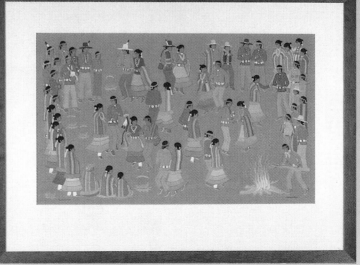

Arugula Salad
with Smoked Pheasant, Raspberries, and Red Onions

Yield: 4 servings

Arugula — also known as rocket — is a member of the cabbage family that has recently become very popular. Its slightly peppery, sharp flavor perfectly matches those of the smoked pheasant and raspberry vinaigrette. Arugula should be washed well as the leaves are often sandy or gritty and used as soon as possible after purchase as it does not keep well.

Meat of ¹/₂ smoked pheasant
  (or 1¹/₂ cups, about 5 ounces,
  smoked chicken or turkey),
  julienned
1 red onion, thinly sliced

1 cup fresh raspberries
8 ounces (2 bunches, trimmed)
  arugula
Raspberry Vinaigrette
  (recipe follows)

Combine the pheasant, onion, berries and arugula in a large mixing bowl. Toss with the raspberry vinaigrette.

Raspberry Vinaigrette   Yield: about 1¹/₃ cups

¹/₃ cup raspberry vinegar
1 teaspoon Dijon mustard
1 tablespoon chopped mixed fresh
  herbs, such as parsley, chives,
  basil, and oregano

1 cup olive oil
Salt and freshly ground pepper
  to taste

Place the vinegar in a mixing bowl, add the mustard and herbs, and mix together. Gradually whisk in the olive oil, salt, and pepper.

Opposite page:
Santa Fe Fruit Salad,
page 100.

O'Keeffe Salad
with Honey and Poppyseed Dressing

Yield: 4 servings

This salad, one of the prettiest you'll ever see, is reminiscent of a painting by New Mexico's most famous artist, Georgia O'Keeffe. It was designed by a well-known artist in Santa Fe who would probably like to remain anonymous in the gustatory field.

16 leaves Napa (Chinese) cabbage
16 spears Belgian endive
4 rings (about $\frac{1}{3}$-inch thick) cantaloupe melon, rind removed
4 rings red bell pepper
$\frac{1}{2}$ cup Honey and Poppyseed Dressing (recipe follows)
4 nasturtiums, for garnish

On each serving plate, arrange 4 leaves of the Napa cabbage like a four-leafed clover. Place a spear of Belgian endive on top of each cabbage leaf. Place the cantaloupe rings in the middle to cover the inside edges of the cabbage leaves, and place the smaller ring of bell pepper inside the cantaloupe.

Pour 2 tablespoons of the dressing over each salad and garnish with a nasturtium.

Honey and Poppyseed Dressing   Yield: about $\frac{2}{3}$ cup

$\frac{1}{2}$ tablespoon Dijon mustard
1 tablespoon honey
2 tablespoons white wine vinegar
2 tablespoons canola oil
$\frac{1}{4}$ cup extra virgin olive oil
$\frac{1}{2}$ tablespoon poppyseeds
Salt and freshly ground pepper to taste

In a blender, combine the mustard, honey, and vinegar. With the blender running, gradually add both oils in a steady stream until the mixture has emulsified. Pour the dressing into a bowl, add the poppyseeds, and season with salt and pepper.

Zia Salad
with Nuts and Cranberry and Walnut Vinaigrette

Yield: 4 servings

The *zia* is an ancient symbol used by the native Americans of the Southwest, and it dominates the New Mexico state flag. It is variously said to represent the four points of the compass, the four seasons, or the four stages of man, or all of these. The strips of jícama suggesting the zia symbol make this another striking salad.

Use whichever greens you like best or look freshest for this recipe. You can use a sundried tomato and sage dressing (page 101) instead of this cranberry and walnut vinaigrette, if you prefer.

³⁄₄ cup toasted piñones (pine nut)
³⁄₄ cup toasted sunflower seeds
¹⁄₄ cup toasted unsweetened coconut
³⁄₄ cup toasted, sliced unblanched almonds

Mixed greens, such as mustard greens, mâche, and fresh sage
¹⁄₂ small jícama, peeled and cut into 48 thin, 3-inch long strips
Cranberry Walnut Vinaigrette (recipe follows)

To prepare the nut salad, toss all the ingredients with ¾ cup of the vinaigrette. Arrange the salad on serving plates. To make the zia pattern, place 3 parallel strips of jícama (arrayed from the middle of the plate outward) at the 4 points of the compass on the outside of each plate as in the illustration. Serve the remaining vinaigrette on the side.

Cranberry and Walnut Vinaigrette   Yield: about 3 cups

¹⁄₄ cup fresh cranberries
¹⁄₂ cup water
¹⁄₄ cup walnut oil
¹⁄₄ cup Mayonnaise (page 161)
Juice of 2 oranges
Juice of 2 limes
1¹⁄₂ teaspoons chopped fresh sage

¹⁄₄ cup red wine vinegar
³⁄₄ cup heavy cream
2 tablespoons pure red chile powder
1 tablespoon chopped garlic
Salt to taste

Simmer the cranberries and water for 2 minutes, drain, and purée in a blender. Add all the remaining ingredients and blend together. Let the dressing sit in the refrigerator overnight for the flavors to meld.

House Salad
with Mayfair Dressing

Yield: 4 servings

The Mayfair Dressing is a classic that was created back in the 1950s when I owned the Mayfair Hotel in St. Louis. Recently, the *St. Louis Post-Dispatch* accurately reported that the dressing had attracted national attention. The new owners asked me and I agreed to share the recipe as a contribution to the hotel's resurrection.

The dressing makes an excellent dip when mixed with equal parts of mayonnaise. This recipe makes four small side salads. Increase the quantities if you want more substantial servings.

½ head (about 4 ounces) Bibb lettuce
2 tomatoes, cut into 12 wedges
4 ounces (2¼ cups) thinly sliced mushrooms

4 tablespoons sunflower seeds
¾ cup Mayfair Dressing (recipe follows)

Arrange the lettuce on small salad plates, with the tomato wedges set around the edge. Place the mushrooms and sunflower seeds on top and sprinkle the dressing over the salads to taste.

Mayfair Dressing   Yield: about 1¼ cups

¼ onion, roughly chopped
½ stick celery
2 ounces (1 can) anchovies
1 clove garlic
1 extra-large egg

1 tablespoon mustard
¼ cup water
1 cup olive oil
½ teaspoon freshly ground black pepper

Place all the ingredients in a blender and blend until they are smooth.

Jícama Slaw
with Soy Vinaigrette and
Honey and Lemon Dressing

Yield: 4 servings

Jícama is a turnip-shaped tuber that has the crisp, crunchy texture and flavor of a water chestnut, only sweeter. It is native to Mexico and has only been introduced to the United States relatively recently. It can be cooked, but jícama is particularly refreshing served raw and makes a great ingredient in salads and salsas. In this recipe, the sweetness and crunch of the jícama and carrot contrast intriguingly and deliciously with the sharpness of the radicchio and endive.

2 cups julienned jícama
1/4 cup julienned carrot
1 red bell pepper, julienned
1/2 bunch chives, cut into 1-inch lengths (about 1/4 cup)
1 cup Soy Vinaigrette (page 96)
4 large radicchio leaves
8 large Belgian endive leaves

1 cup Honey and Lemon Dressing (recipe follows)
2 small avocados, peeled, pitted, and thinly sliced, for garnish
1 lemon, peeled and thinly sliced, for garnish

In a mixing bowl, toss together the jícama, carrot, bell pepper, chives, and vinaigrette. Let the mixture marinate at room temperature for 1 hour.

Toss the radicchio and endive in the Honey and Lemon Dressing, arrange on serving plates, and add the marinated ingredients on top. Garnish the salad with the avocado and lemon slices.

Honey and Lemon Dressing Yield: about 1 1/2 cups

1 cup heavy cream
2 tablespoons clover honey
1/4 bunch parsley, chopped
1/4 teaspoon fresh lime juice
Juice of 2 lemons

1/4 teaspoon lemon zest
1/4 teaspoon chopped mint
Salt to taste
1/4 teaspoon freshly ground black pepper

Place all the ingredients in a blender, purée them, and chill the dressing.

Grilled Snapper Salad
with Soy Vinaigrette

Yield: 4 servings

This salad makes the perfect summer lunch. You can use a different fish, such as rockfish or monkfish, if you prefer. Likewise, use whichever lettuces look freshest.

1 recipe Soy Marinade for Fish (page 164)
4 red snapper or rockfish fillets, about 6 ounces each

Soy Vinaigrette (recipe follows)
8 ounces mixed green lettuces

Prepare the marinade, allowing time for it to cool. When it is cool, transfer the marinade to a mixing bowl and marinate the fish in it for between 15 and 20 minutes at room temperature.

While the fish is marinating, prepare the vinaigrette.

Remove the fish from the marinade and grill the fillets over medium heat for between 3 and 5 minutes per side. Toss the lettuces with the vinaigrette and place them on serving plates. Put the grilled fish on top.

Soy Vinaigrette   Yield: about ¼ cup

2 tablespoons rice wine vinegar
2 tablespoons soy sauce
2 tablespoons fresh lemon juice
2 tablespoons minced ginger
1 tablespoon minced garlic

2 tablespoons minced scallions
½ teaspoon chile caribe (dried red chile flakes)
¼ cup olive oil

Thoroughly combine all the ingredients in a mixing bowl.

Red Chile Pesto and Pasta Salad

Yield: 4 servings

The Chimayó chile, like some other red chiles from northern New Mexico, is a subspecies that has never been subject to cross-pollination because of its relative isolation from the main chile growing areas to the south. This, together with the microclimate and soil conditions peculiar to the high mountain valleys such as Chimayó, give these chiles distinctive qualities of heat and flavor. Similar varieties of grapes grown in different locations also display unique characteristics.

This Southwestern pesto makes a welcome — and *picante* — change in the classic pasta salad.

Red Chile Pesto   Yield: about 4 cups

6 cloves garlic
½ cup piñones (pine nuts)
½ cup freshly grated Parmesan cheese
1 bunch cilantro, leaves only, chopped
¾ cup firmly packed basil leaves

¼ cup pure red chile powder (preferably Chimayó or New Mexico)
¼ cup chile caribe (dried red chile flakes)
2 teaspoons ground cumin
Salt to taste
2 cups olive oil

1 pound (about 6 cups) fusilli (spiral pasta)
8 to 12 red oak-leaf lettuce leaves,

16 pitted calamata olives, for garnish
1 yellow bell pepper, seeded and julienned, for garnish

To make the pesto, place all the ingredients except for the olive oil in a food processor and purée them. With the machine running, gradually drizzle in the oil and blend until it is thoroughly emulsified.

In a large pan of boiling water, cook the pasta until *al dente*, about 5 minutes. Drain it and rinse it in cold water. Mix the cooked pasta and about half of the pesto in a large mixing bowl. Taste the mixture and add more pesto until the flavors are nicely balanced. (Refrigerate any leftover pesto.) Serve the pasta over a bed of lettuce and garnish with the olives and yellow bell pepper.

Cold Pasta Salad
with Smoked Salmon

Yield: 4 servings

Make sure you use a really good quality smoked salmon for this recipe. We prefer the northern European varieties — Scottish, Irish, or Scandinavian — which are cold-smoked Atlantic (rather than Pacific) salmon. Nova Scotia salmon has improved in quality, but avoid the brine-cured and cold-smoked lox type of salmon that is sometimes quite salty. With smoked salmon, as with so many other things in life, "you gets what you pays for."

½ cup plus 1 tablespoon olive oil
2 tablespoons fresh lemon juice
1 shallot, finely chopped
½ cup chopped fresh dill
8 ounces (about 4 cups) penne pasta, or pasta of choice

6 ounces sliced smoked salmon, julienned
1 cup cherry tomatoes, cut in half
½ red onion, thinly sliced

In a small bowl, mix together the ½ cup olive oil, lemon juice, shallot, and dill, and set aside.

Cook the pasta until *al dente*. Rinse it under cold water, drain it, add the remaining tablespoon of olive oil, and toss. Let the pasta cool to room temperature.

Add the reserved oil and lemon juice mixture and the salmon, tomatoes, and onion to the pasta and mix the ingredients together delicately.

Chicken Salad in a Pineapple

Yield: 4 servings

This is a spectacular summer luncheon salad, especially if you keep the leaves attached to the pineapple; carefully cut the crown of leaves in half when slicing the pineapple lengthwise. Feel free to substitute your favorite salad ingredients and whichever fruit is in season or that you prefer.

1 chicken, about 3 pounds

4 cloves

1 onion, cut in half

2 carrots, thinly sliced

1 bay leaf

10 peppercorns

2 stalks celery, cut in half lengthwise and thinly sliced

1/4 cup raisins

1/4 cup chopped water chestnuts

1/4 cup Mayonnaise (page 161)

Salt and freshly ground pepper to taste

2 pineapples, cut in half lengthwise, crown of leaves attached

Fresh fruit, such as grapes, banana slices, and wedges of kiwi fruit and orange, for garnish

Place the chicken in a large, heavy-bottomed pot, cover it with water, and bring the water to a boil. Skim the surface and reduce the heat to a simmer. Stick the cloves into the onion halves and add them to the pot, together with the carrots, bay leaf, and peppercorns. Cover the pot and simmer the chicken for 50 minutes. Remove the chicken and let it cool. Remove the meat from the chicken and dice it into 1/4-inch cubes.

In a mixing bowl, thoroughly combine the diced chicken, celery, raisins, water chestnuts, and mayonnaise. Season with salt and pepper.

Core the pineapple halves, and scoop out a little of the flesh. Place the pineapple halves on serving plates and fill them with the chicken salad. Garnish with the fresh fruit.

Santa Fe Fruit Salad
with Apricot and Yogurt Dressing

Yield: 4 servings

You may use different fruits depending on the season and your personal preference. The three important things to remember are: use only fresh fruit, use at least five varieties of fruit, and cut the fruit artistically and arrange it on the plate with as much thought as you'd give to arranging a vase of flowers.

1 pineapple, peeled, cored, quartered, and cut into ¹/₂ -inch slices

2 apples, halved, cored, and thinly sliced

1 cantaloupe melon, quartered and cut into wedges

1 orange, peeled and cut into rings

1 pint strawberries, washed and stemmed

Apricot and Yogurt Dressing (recipe follows)

Arrange the fruit on serving plates, with the Apricot and Yogurt Dressing on the side.

Apricot and Yogurt Dressing Yield: about 1½ cups

12 dried apricots

2 tablespoons water

1 cup plain yogurt

In a mixing bowl, soak the dried apricots in hot water for 20 minutes. When they are rehydrated, transfer the apricots to a blender and purée them with the 2 tablespoons water until smooth. Blend the apricot purée with the yogurt.

Sundried Tomato and Pine Nut Vinaigrette

Yield: about 2 cups

Use this dressing with leaf lettuces, Romaine, or spinach salads.

³⁄₄ cup toasted piñones (pine nuts)
¹⁄₂ cup sundried tomatoes (packed in oil), chopped
6 fresh sage leaves
1 clove garlic, peeled
¹⁄₂ teaspoon pure chile powder
Juice of 1 lemon

¹⁄₃ cup red wine vinegar
¹⁄₂ cup olive oil
¹⁄₂ cup canola oil
1 teaspoon salt
1 teaspoon freshly ground black pepper

Place half of the pine nuts in a blender with the sundried tomatoes, sage, garlic, chile powder, lemon juice, and vinegar, and chop. With the blender running, gradually drizzle in the oils in a steady stream and blend until the mixture has emulsified. Add the remaining pine nuts and season with salt and pepper.

Creamy Sundried Tomato and Sage Dressing

Yield: about 2 cups

Use an orange chile powder for a more striking presentation. This dressing is an excellent accompaniment for pasta salads, and is best made a day ahead.

¹⁄₄ cup sundried tomatoes, rehydrated in hot water, drained and puréed
¹⁄₂ tablespoon chopped fresh sage
¹⁄₂ cup Mayonnaise (page 161)
¹⁄₄ teaspoon chopped garlic
Juice of 2 oranges

Juice of 2 limes
¹⁄₄ cup red wine vinegar
³⁄₄ cup heavy cream
2 tablespoons pure red chile powder
Salt to taste

Thoroughly blend all the ingredients together in a blender or by hand.

Walnut Oil and Balsamic Vinegar Dressing

Yield: about 1½ cups

Use with mixed green salads.

⅓ cup balsamic vinegar
1 teaspoon Dijon mustard
1 tablespoon chopped shallots
Salt and freshly ground pepper
   to taste

Paprika to taste
½ cup olive oil
½ cup walnut oil

Place the vinegar in a mixing bowl, and stir in the mustard and shallots. Season with salt, pepper, and paprika. Gradually whisk in the olive oil and then the walnut oil in a steady stream.

Fish & Seafood

*A*lthough modern airfreight has greatly reduced the time it takes to get fresh fish to the table, the process of harvesting and marketing still extends that time beyond the optimum. Most trawlers stay at sea for about ten days, and the secret is to buy the fish caught on the last day. Smell is the most reliable method of selection, so use your nose: fish should not smell too fishy, instead they should have a fresh aroma of the sea. Whole fish keep better than filleted fish do; their freshness is also easier to judge. The skin, like the eyes, should be bright and shiny; if the eyes are cloudy or no longer convex, the fish is old. The lungs under the gills should be bright pink or red, not white.

At La Casa Sena, we pay top prices for the freshest fish and seafood, and we check the quality very carefully. Woe betide the supplier who sends a suspicious shipment, as it will be returned and the supplier blacklisted for a period of time that fits the severity of the crime! This policy is one reason that you will generally eat better seafood at La Casa Sena than at home.

Most people routinely overcook fish, which is a shame as the texture and flavor both suffer. A good rule of thumb is to cook fish quickly, over high heat, and to cook it for ten minutes per inch of thickness.

In the recipes that follow, we have used the most common names for each type of fish, but bear in mind that there are countless regional variations in the names of just about every fish in the sea. Many fish are renamed purely for marketing reasons. The best example of this is the red snapper, which is truly a Gulf and Caribbean fish. The Pacific snapper is native to the Micronesian islands. However, in the state of California numerous species, among them grouper and seabass, may legally be marketed as red snapper. *Caveat emptor!*

A view of the west entrance to the enclosed courtyard of Sena Plaza in 1920.

Grilled Mahi-Mahi
with Vegetable Purée and Leek and Jalapeño Sauce

Yield: 4 servings

Mahi-mahi is another name for the dolphinfish (not to be confused with the lovable mammal, which is quite different). This confusion is one reason why the name mahi-mahi — the Hawaiian term — is most commonly used. Mahi-mahi is a warm water fish found around the world, and it also happens to be one of the more beautiful of edible fishes.

Vegetable Purée

2 carrots, peeled and sliced

6 to 8 medium potatoes (about 2 pounds), peeled and cut into ¹/₂-inch cubes

2 rutabagas or turnips, peeled and cut into ¹/₂-inch cubes

1 yellow onion, chopped

2 cloves garlic, chopped

1 teaspoon ground allspice

1 teaspoon freshly ground white pepper

2 teaspoons salt

Leek and Jalapeño Sauce (recipe follows)

4 mahi-mahi filets, about 6 ounces each

To make the purée, place the carrots, potatoes, rutabagas, onion, and garlic in a large saucepan, cover them with water, and bring to a boil. Reduce the heat and simmer until the vegetables are soft, about 45 minutes. Drain and reserve a little of the cooking liquid. Transfer the vegetables to a food processor or blender, and purée them with a little of the cooking liquid if necessary. Stir in the allspice, pepper, and salt.

Meanwhile, prepare the grill or broiler. Over medium heat, grill (or broil) the mahi-mahi until it is cooked through, 3 to 5 minutes per side.

Place the puréed vegetables on the center of each serving plate, place the mahi-mahi on top, and serve the sauce around the vegetables.

Leek and Jalapeño Sauce   Yield: about 2 cups

4 cups chicken or vegetable stock

2 leeks, white part only, finely diced

2 jalapeños chiles, seeded and finely diced

Salt and freshly ground white pepper to taste

Place the stock, leeks, and jalapeños in a saucepan and, over medium-high heat, reduce the liquid by half. Season with salt and pepper.

Opposite page: Pan-Seared Tuna with Spanish Rice and Tomatillo Salsa, page 107.

Canyon de Chelly
Fremont Ellis

Pueblo Scene
Albert Schmidt

The Bread Ovens
Henry Balink

Spring in Pojoaque
Randall Davey

Untitled
Ward Lockwood

Landscape
Carlos Vierra

Pan-Seared Tuna
with Spanish Rice and Tomatillo Salsa

Yield: 4 servings

Tuna is a member of the mackerel family, and there are several varieties, including yellowfin, bluefin (the largest), albacore, and the much smaller bonito.

The tomatillo salsa is a good all-purpose salsa that goes beautifully with almost any seafood.

4 cups Spanish Rice (page 169)
2 cups Tomatillo Salsa
(recipe follows)
4 tuna fillets, about 6 ounces each

Salt and freshly ground
black pepper to taste
2 tablespoons olive oil

Prepare the rice and salsa.

Season the tuna fillets with salt and pepper, and heat the oil in a non-stick sauté pan. Sauté the fish over medium-high heat until the fillets are brown and crispy but still moist, about 3 or 4 minutes per side for medium rare.

Serve the tuna with the rice and salsa, and a seasonal vegetable, such as zucchini or asparagus, if desired.

Tomatillo Salsa   Yield: about 2 cups

6 tomatillos, roasted (see page 163)
and chopped
1/2 cup diced fresh pineapple
1/2 cup diced red onion
1/4 cup diced red bell pepper
3 tablespoons chopped
fresh cilantro

5 tablespoons fresh orange juice
2 tablespoons fresh lime juice
2 tablespoons white vinegar
Salt and freshly ground pepper
to taste

In a large glass or ceramic mixing bowl, thoroughly combine all the ingredients. Keep the salsa cool in the refrigerator.

Opposite page:
Grilled Swordfish
with Sauteéd Apples
and Onions and Plum
and Orange Sauce,
page 111. The bottle of
Chardonnay shows a
label by Wayne Thiebaud.

Grilled Ahi Tuna
with Asparagus and Mango and Lime Salsa

Yield: 4 servings

Just as *mahi-mahi* is Hawaiian for the dolphinfish, *ahi* is Hawaiian for the albacore or yellowfin tuna, which is native to the warm waters of Hawaii and the Pacific. The ahi ranges from seventy-five to two hundred pounds (small-fry compared with the bluefin variety which can reach one thousand pounds), and is usually fished with a line in the deep sea. Ahi are at their peak during the summer, from May through August.

Mango and Lime Salsa
   (recipe follows)
2 tablespoons olive oil
1 pound asparagus, sliced into
   $^1/_2$-inch pieces
$^1/_2$ cup chicken or vegetable stock

Juice of 2 limes
1 tablespoon honey
$^1/_2$ bunch cilantro, minced
4 ahi tuna fillets, about
   6 ounces each

Prepare the salsa and set it aside.

Heat the olive oil in a saucepan and over medium high heat, sauté the asparagus for 2 to 3 minutes. Add the stock, lime juice, honey, and cilantro, and cook for a further 2 to 3 minutes.

Meanwhile, prepare the grill or broiler. Over medium heat, grill (or broil) the tuna until the fillets are cooked through, between 3 and 5 minutes per side.

Place some of the asparagus on the center of each serving plate and spoon the liquid around it. Place the tuna on top of the asparagus and serve the salsa at the side.

Mango and Lime Salsa   Yield: about 3 cups

4 mangoes, peeled, pitted, and cut
   into $^1/_8$-inch cubes
4 limes, peeled and cut
   into segments

2 jalapeño chiles, seeded
   and finely chopped
2 tablespoons white wine vinegar

Place all the ingredients in a saucepan and simmer for between 15 and 20 minutes. Add a little water if necessary. Let the salsa cool.

Seared Salmon
with Celery Root Purée
and Red Wine and Shallot Sauce

Yield: 4 servings

Almost all North American salmon is caught in the Pacific, and mostly in Alaskan waters. Fresh salmon, be it Coho, Chinook, Sockeye, or any of the many other species, is one of the finest foods available from the sea. One reason it tastes so good is because it has a relatively high fat content. The good news is that these fats are predominantly of the omega-3 variety, one of the beneficial types.

Celery root, or celeriac, comes from a special type of celery grown just for the root, and is in season mostly during the winter.

Celery Root Purée

2 celery roots, peeled and cut into 1-inch cubes

2 medium baking potatoes, peeled and cut into 1-inch cubes

¹⁄₂ cup heavy cream

2 tablespoons unsalted butter

Salt and freshly ground pepper to taste

Red Wine and Shallot Sauce   Yield: about 2 cups

8 shallots, finely diced

3 cups Cabernet Sauvignon wine (we use J. Lohr Estates Seven Oaks)

4 tablespoons unsalted butter (or more, to taste)

Salt and freshly ground pepper to taste

2 tablespoons olive oil

4 salmon fillets, about 6 ounces each

Salt and freshly ground pepper to taste

To prepare the celery root purée, bring a saucepan of lightly salted water to a boil and cook the celery and potato for 30 minutes, or until tender. Drain the water and mash the vegetables. Add the cream, thoroughly mix together, and heat through. Mix in the butter and season with salt and pepper.

To prepare the sauce, bring the shallots and wine to a boil in a saucepan and reduce by half. Remove the pan from the heat and whisk in the butter, 1 tablespoon at a time, to taste. Season with salt and pepper.

To prepare the salmon, heat the olive oil in a skillet or pan, season the fillets with salt and pepper, and sauté them for 3 to 5 minutes per side.

Place the celery root purée in the center of the serving plates, surround it with the sauce, and place the salmon on the purée.

Grilled Salmon
with Golden Tomato and Cucumber Relish

Yield: 6 servings

The salmon found in the cooler waters of the Atlantic is pinker than that found in the Pacific, which tends to be darker red. Salmon has a wonderfully delicate and distinctive flavor, and its firm texture always makes fresh salmon a delight to eat. Hothouse or English cucumbers, which have the advantage of containing very few seeds, can grow up to two feet in length.

Golden Tomato and Cucumber Relish   Yield: about 6 cups

1 pint basket (2-2½ cups) yellow pear tomatoes, or red cherry tomatoes, cut in half lengthwise

1 medium hothouse cucumber, seeded and cut into ¾-inch dice

2 bunches (about 1 cup) opal (purple) basil, or fresh sweet basil, stemmed and finely chopped

¼ bunch (about 2 tablespoons) fresh peppermint, stemmed and finely chopped

½ cup sherry vinegar

1½ cups olive oil

2 shallots, peeled and finely chopped

1 bunch chives, chopped (about ½ cup)

Salt and freshly ground pepper to taste

❖

6 salmon steaks, about 6 ounces each

2 tablespoons olive oil

To make the relish, place the tomatoes and cucumber in a mixing bowl. Add the basil, mint, vinegar, oil, shallots, and chives, and mix gently. Season with salt and pepper

Lightly oil the salmon and place the steaks on a hot grill. Cook both sides until done, about 5 or 6 minutes per side. Remove the fish from the grill and transfer it to serving plates. Spoon the relish over each portion and serve immediately.

Seared Swordfish
with Sautéed Apples and Onions
and Plum and Orange Sauce

Yield: 4 servings

Swordfish are found mostly in warmer seas and average between four hundred and five hundred pounds. They are striking-looking creatures, with large fins and their swordlike "noses," but as they are so large, we only ever see them as steaks, which seems a shame. Commercial fishermen used to locate schools of swordfish with spotter planes, but this practice has now been banned.

Orchards of plums can be found up and down the Rio Grande valley in northern New Mexico. We use a Grenache wine for the fruity sauce, but Pinot Noir will also work well.

Plum and Orange Sauce   Yield: about 4 cups

1 pound plums, pitted and puréed

1½ cups fresh orange juice

¼ cup red wine, preferably Grenache or Pinot Noir

½ cup vegetable or fish stock

2 cloves garlic, minced

3 tablespoons minced shallots

½ cup minced fresh basil leaves

---

2 tablespoons butter

4 apples, cored and cut in 6 wedges each

3 onions, thinly sliced

2 cups red wine

3 tablespoons sugar

1 tablespoon cider vinegar

¼ cup seedless raisins

Salt and freshly ground pepper to taste

4 swordfish fillets, 6 ounces each

2 tablespoons olive oil

To prepare the sauce, place all the ingredients in a saucepan and bring to a boil. Reduce the heat and simmer slowly for between 15 and 20 minutes.

Heat the butter in a skillet and sauté the apple wedges until they are tender, about 5 minutes. Place the onions, wine, sugar, and vinegar in a saucepan and cook over medium heat until almost all the liquid has evaporated. Stir in the raisins, and season with salt and pepper.

Season the swordfish fillets with salt and pepper, and heat the oil in a nonstick sauté pan. Sauté the fish over medium-high heat until the fillets are brown and crispy but still moist, between 3 and 4 minutes per side for medium rare. Serve the swordfish with the apples and onions, and pour the sauce around.

Grilled Swordfish
with Lentils and Tomatillo Salsa

Yield: 4 servings

Swordfish tend to be seasonal and can be bought fresh during the summer; during the rest of the year, they are likely to be frozen. Because their flesh is firm and mild tasting, it is best to pair swordfish with assertive flavors and different textures. The combination in this recipe works very well.

1 pound green or red lentils
2 cups chicken or vegetable stock
2 cups water
4 tablespoons olive oil
1 yellow onion, finely chopped
2 carrots, finely chopped
1 stick celery, finely chopped
3 cloves garlic, finely chopped

1 teaspoon chopped fresh parsley
1 teaspoon chopped fresh thyme
4 swordfish steaks, about 6 ounces each
Salt and freshly ground pepper to taste
¹/₂ cup Tomatillo Salsa (page 107)

Place the lentils in a saucepan with enough water to cover them by 1 inch, bring to a boil, and immediately drain the lentils and rinse them under cold water. Transfer the lentils to a clean pan with the stock and 2 cups water, bring the mixture to a boil, and simmer for 35 minutes. When cooked, drain the lentils.

Heat 2 tablespoons of the olive oil in a saucepan with a heavy bottom and sauté the onion, carrots, celery, and garlic with the parsley and thyme for 3 to 5 minutes. Add the lentils and stir together to combine.

Brush the swordfish steaks with the remaining olive oil and season them with salt and pepper. Grill for 4 to 5 minutes per side.

To serve, place some of the lentil mixture on the center of each plate. Place the swordfish on the center of the lentils, and serve the salsa at the side.

Braid of Three Fish
with Shellfish and Chive Sauce

Yield: 4 servings.

This dish not only looks spectacular, with the braiding of three different colored fish, but also the different flavors give it a unique taste. You can experiment with different sauces if you prefer, or none at all. The only potential problem with this culinary masterpiece is that your dinner guests are likely never to invite you back to their house after they witness your intimidating prowess.

Chive Sauce   Yield: about 1⅔ cups

1 cup Mayonnaise (page 161)
⅓ cup fish stock or clam juice

Juice of ½ lemon
¼ cup finely chopped fresh chives

1 leek
8 ounces salmon fillet in 1 piece
8 ounces mahi-mahi fillet
  in 1 piece
8 ounces swordfish fillet in 1 piece
8 shrimp, peeled

8 mussels
8 clams
2 cups court bouillon (page 164),
  prepared — note that it takes
  45 minutes to cook — and set
  aside

Preheat the oven to 350°F.

To prepare the sauce, place all the ingredients in a saucepan and heat them gradually over low heat. Do not let the sauce boil.

Cut the leek to a length of 8 inches, and then cut it in half lengthwise. Blanch the pieces in boiling water for 2 or 3 minutes, and then plunge them into ice water. When cool, cut the leek into ⅛-inch strips.

Cut each fish fillet into 4 thin strips. Using 1 strand of each variety, make 4 braids of the strips of fish. Use the strips of leek to tie the ends of the braids. Place the fish braids on a buttered ovenproof dish, sprinkle with a little water, and bake them in the oven for 5 minutes.

Meanwhile, in a pan, poach the shrimp and shellfish in the *court bouillon*, simmering them gently for between 5 and 6 minutes. When cooked, remove the top shell of the mussels and clams.

Place the fish braids on serving plates with the chive sauce. Arrange the shrimp, mussels, and clams, moistened with a little of the poaching liquid, on the side.

Roasted Halibut
with Sautéed Red Potatoes and Leeks and Tartar Sauce

Yield: 4 servings

In general, the colder the water, the firmer the flesh of the fish; so the best halibut is found in more northern waters, from Newfoundland and Greenland to Norway; in the north Pacific; and in the Barents Sea off Russia. Halibut is a flat fish with firm, white, flesh and relatively little fat. It is available both as fillets and steaks, and has a mild, delicate flavor. Usually available year round, it tends to be more plentiful during the summer months.

4 tablespoons clarified butter

6 leeks, white part only, thinly sliced

12 new red potatoes, cooked and cut into ¼-inch slices

4 halibut fillets, about 6 ounces each

Salt and freshly ground pepper to taste

1 cup Tartar Sauce (page 160)

Heat 2 tablespoons of the clarified butter in a large pan and sauté the leeks over medium heat for 5 minutes. Add the potatoes and sauté them for 5 minutes longer, gently stirring occasionally so that the vegetables cook evenly.

Meanwhile, in a large sauté pan or skillet, heat the remaining 2 tablespoons of clarified butter over medium-high heat. Season the halibut with salt and pepper, and sauté the fillets for 3 or 4 minutes on each side. Serve with the vegetables and tartar sauce on the side.

Sautéed Rockfish
with Scallion and Potato Purée
and Whole-Grain Mustard Sauce

Yield: 4 servings

Rockfish is a Pacific species that is sometimes referred to as Pacific snapper; it is not, however, related to the true red snapper which comes from the Atlantic, although they are interchangeable. Rockfish can be bought whole (they average between five and ten pounds), but you may find it easier and more expedient to have the fish market filet it for you.

The flavored potato purée and the mustard sauce contrast perfectly with the delicate, firm flesh of the fish.

Scallion and Potato Purée

8 baking potatoes, peeled and diced into 1-inch cubes
2 tablespoons salt

1 cup half-and-half
¹/₂ cup olive oil
8 scallions, very thinly sliced

Whole-Grain Mustard Sauce   Yield: about 2 cups

1 tablespoon butter
4 shallots, finely diced
1 cup white wine

1 tablespoon butter
¹/₂ cup all-purpose flour

1 cup fish stock or chicken stock
¹/₂ cup whole-grain mustard
1 cup heavy cream

4 rockfish fillets, about 6 ounces each

To make the purée, place the potatoes in a large saucepan, cover them with water, add the salt, and bring to a boil. Reduce the heat and simmer gently until the potatoes are soft, about 25 to 30 minutes.

Meanwhile, heat the half-and-half in a pan until it is hot but not boiling. Drain the potatoes, return them to the pan, and add the hot half-and-half and the olive oil. Mash the potatoes, adding the sliced scallions.

To make the mustard sauce, heat the 1 tablespoon butter in a saucepan, and sauté the shallots over medium heat until they are soft, about 2 minutes. Add the wine, bring it to a boil, add the stock, and reduce the liquid by half. Add the mustard and cream, and reduce until the sauce is thick and creamy.

Heat 1 tablespoon of butter in a large sauté pan or skillet. Dust the rockfish in the flour and sauté for 4 to 5 minutes per side over medium heat.

Divide the purée evenly among the serving plates, pour the sauce around, and place the rockfish on top of the purée.

Trucha en Terracota
Trout Wrapped in Clay

Yield: 4 servings

This is one of the most exciting dinners anyone could have. Hollywood found it so impressive that a segment of *White Sands* was filmed in our courtyard just so a waiter could be shown breaking open the adobe clay and serving the cooked trout within. Unfortunately, the director insisted that one of the cast act the part of the waiter: his swings at the thing made it look like an axe murder rather than a fine-dining experience. The trick is to take two large service spoons and tap the baked clay with gentle drumlike smacks to crack it. Then, the trout can be removed and the grape leaves folded back to expose the fish. The leaves give a marvelous pungency to the meat and can be eaten. Use the preserved grape leaves that come in glass jars. You'll find them in most gourmet stores and the clay in an art supply store.

4 slices of rolled red clay, ¼-inch thick (about 1 pound of clay per slice)
40 grape leaves, rinsed
2 hardboiled eggs, finely chopped
4 ounces (about ⅔ cup) smoked salmon, finely chopped
2 tablespoons chopped fresh parsley
2 tablespoons chopped fresh dill
2 tablespoons chopped fresh chives
2 tablespoons chopped shallots
¼ cup Crème Fraîche (page 161)
4 boneless trout, about 8 ounces each
Lemon wedges and parsley springs, for garnish

Preheat the oven to 400°F.

Roll the slices of clay between sheets of parchment paper until they are large ovals about 10 by 12 inches in size. Arrange 10 of the grape leaves out in the shape of the trout on each clay slice so that there are no spaces between the leaves.

Thoroughly mix together the eggs, smoked salmon, herbs, shallots, and crème fraîche, and stuff about 2 tablespoons, or as much as will fit, in each trout. Wrap the stuffed trout in the grape leaves so that no skin shows through. Fold the clay over and mold it to the outline of the fish. Mark the clay with patterns resembling a fish: eyes, fins, and scales.

Bake the fish in the oven (either on a baking sheet or directly on the rack), for 30 to 40 minutes or until the clay is dry. Serve on a platter and gently break the clay open at the table, using two large spoons like drumsticks. Carefully remove the trout, transfer to dinner plates. Fold back the grape leaves and garnish with lemon wedges and parsley.

Red Snapper
with Gazpacho Sauce and Ratatouille

Yield: 4 servings

There are many varieties of snapper (their colorful prefixes include "schoolmaster" and "mutton" snapper) and, despite the interesting imagery these types may conjure up, the best-known and loved variety is the red snapper. It is native to the warm waters of the Gulf of Mexico and the Atlantic coast of the southeast United States, where it is one of the most significant catches, in terms of numbers and marketability. The red snapper's firm flesh is low in fat, and its delicate flavor is superior to that of other types of snapper.

Gazpacho Sauce   Yield: about 2½ cups

1 pound (about 3 cups) cherry tomatoes
⅓ cup white wine vinegar
1 teaspoon salt
1 teaspoon sugar
½ teaspoon freshly ground white pepper
⅓ cup olive oil

Ratatouille

2 tablespoons olive oil
3 cloves garlic, minced
½ red onion, finely chopped
1 small zucchini, finely chopped (about 1 cup)
1 cup finely chopped eggplant
1 large green bell pepper, seeded and finely chopped
1 large red bell pepper, seeded and finely chopped
2 Roma tomatoes, chopped

4 red snapper fillets, about 6 ounces each
½ cup all-purpose flour
Salt and freshly ground pepper to taste
2 tablespoons olive oil

To prepare the sauce, place all the ingredients in a blender, and blend until smooth.

To prepare the *ratatouille*, heat the olive oil in a skillet or pan, and sauté the vegetables over medium heat for 10 to 15 minutes, until they are tender.

Coat the snapper fillets in the flour and season them with salt and pepper. Heat the oil in a nonstick pan and sauté the fish over medium-high heat for between 2 and 3 minutes per side.

Arrange the fish and the ratatouille on a serving plate and serve the sauce poured half over the snapper and half to the side.

Golden Tilapia
with Piñon and Lime Butter

Yield: 4 servings

Tilapia must be one of the most perfect ecological and nutritional foods. This freshwater fish is very high in protein and very low in fat, and never seems to develop a "fishy" odor or taste. It may be farmed in very little water, and mostly feeds on the algae that grow in ponds. You can substitute red snapper or rockfish if you prefer, or if tilapia is unavailable.

The *piñon* and lime butter may be stored for a week or so in the refrigerator. It is also delicious with grilled pork tenderloin medallions and grilled or broiled chicken.

8 tilapia fillets	*2 tablespoons melted butter*
Salt and freshly ground black pepper to taste	*Lemon and lime slices, for garnish*

Piñon and Lime Butter   Yield: about 1 cup

¹/₄ cup toasted piñones (pine nuts)	*1 tablespoon finely chopped parsley*
2 scallions, thinly sliced	
Dash of Worcestershire sauce	*¹/₂ cup (1 stick) softened butter*
¹/₈ teaspoon chile caribe (dried red chile flakes)	*Juice of 1 lime*

Preheat the oven to 350°F.

Place the tilapia fillets in a single layer in a lightly greased baking dish; do not overlap them. Season with salt and pepper. Brush the tops with the melted butter. Bake, uncovered, for about 10 minutes or until the fish flakes when tested with a fork.

Meanwhile, to make the piñon and lime butter, blend the pine nuts, scallions, Worcestershire sauce, chile flakes, parsley, and softened butter. Add the lime juice and salt and pepper to taste, mixing well.

Place 2 tilapia fillets on each serving plate, and top each fillet with about 2 tablespoons of the butter. Garnish with lemon and lime slices.

Rolls of Golden Tilapia
with Tomato and Leeks

Yield: 4 servings

Tilapia was commercially developed originally by the University of Arizona for the Epcot Center, which used the species because it is believed that the Biblical parable of the loaves and fishes was based on it. For this recipe too, you can substitute red snapper or rockfish. The technique used in this dish (which is very popular whenever it appears on the menu at La Casa Sena) is similar to that used for the French *roulade* or *paupiette*.

8 ounces salmon, diced
1 cup heavy cream
1 egg white
Salt and freshly ground pepper to taste
8 tilapia fillets
1 bunch leeks (light green part only), washed and sliced

2 medium tomatoes, seeded and finely diced
½ bunch parsley, finely chopped
1 cup dry white wine
4 tablespoons butter
1 cup thinly sliced mushrooms
1 bunch scallions, thinly sliced

Preheat the oven to 350°F.

Purée the salmon in a food processor until it forms a ball. With the processor running, add the cream, egg white, salt, and pepper, and blend thoroughly. Spread a layer of the salmon mousse on each tilapia fillet.

Place the leeks, tomatoes, parsley, wine, and half the butter in a saucepan. Bring to a boil, reduce the heat and simmer until the leeks are tender, about 10 to 15 minutes. Season with salt and pepper and keep warm.

While the leeks are cooking, melt 2 teaspoons of the remaining butter in a skillet and sauté the mushrooms and scallions until soft. Spread equal portions of the mushroom and scallion mixture on top of the salmon mousse on each fillet. Roll up the fillets, starting at the tails. Arrange the rolls seam side down in a lightly greased baking dish, and season them with salt and pepper. Brush with a small amount of the butter. Bake, uncovered, in the oven for about 10 minutes or until the fish flakes when tested with a fork.

Grilled Sea Scallops
with Lemon Linguine

Yield: 4 servings

Sea scallops are the adductor muscle that hinges the two halves of the beautiful shell of a bivalve mollusc. They are at their peak from around October through April, and should be slightly creamy or pink rather than white (a white hue usually indicates they have been soaked in water to increase their weight). The smaller bay scallops have less intense a flavor and are mostly farmed on the eastern seaboard of the United States.

*1 pound Lemon Linguine
   (recipe follows)*
*20 sea scallops (or 12 to 15 jumbo
   scallops, cut in half cross-wise)*
5 scallions, thinly sliced
*1 pint (2 cups) cherry tomatoes,
   quartered*

*1 jalapeño chile, seeded
   and finely chopped*
*1 bunch basil leaves, julienned
   (about ¹/₂ cup)*
¹/₄ cup olive oil

Make the linguine, allowing time for it to dry.

Prepare the grill. Grill the scallops for 3 to 5 minutes per side.

Cook the linguine in boiling salted water until al dente, 4 or 5 minutes. Drain the linguine and place in a mixing bowl with the scallions, tomatoes, jalapeño, and half of the basil. Add the olive oil, toss the ingredients together, and divide them among the serving plates. Place the grilled scallops on top and sprinkle the remaining basil over the scallops and linguine.

Lemon Linguine   Yield: about 1 pound; 4 servings

4 large eggs, beaten
¹/₂ teaspoon salt
¹/₂ tablespoon olive oil

Juice and zest of ¹/₂ lemon
2 cups (1 pound) durum flour

Mix the eggs, salt, oil, and lemon juice and zest in a mixing bowl. Place the flour in a separate large mixing bowl and form a well in the middle. Add the liquid ingredients and mix until the dough forms a ball. Add a little more flour if necessary. Wrap the dough in plastic and let it rest in the refrigerator for 1 hour.

Transfer the dough to a lightly floured work surface, divide it in half, and roll the pieces out into thin rectangles. Let the sheets dry for between 1 and 2 hours. Gently roll them out again and then cut into strips ¹/₂- to ³/₄-inch wide. Place the strips on parchment paper and let them dry for a further 1 to 2 hours.

Sena Crab Cakes
with Tartar Sauce

Yield: 6 servings

These cakes are best made with blue crab meat, although other varieties (such as Dungeness crab) may also be used. Blue crabs are found on the East Coast and in the Gulf. They shed their shells in late spring and early summer and are then consumed as soft-shell crabs. States surrounding the Chesapeake Bay, such as Maryland and Virginia, are the centers of the blue crab market, and it seems as though natives of this region can wrest all the meat out of one of these small compartmentalized creatures in the time it takes the rest of us to order one from the menu.

1 pound crabmeat
Juice of ½ lemon
1 jalapeño chile, finely chopped
1 leek, white part only, finely diced
½ red bell pepper, peeled, seeded, and diced
3 shallots, diced
1 tablespoon chopped chives
1 tablespoon chopped fresh dill
1 tablespoon chopped fresh parsley

Salt and freshly ground pepper to taste
Cayenne powder to taste
1 tablespoon Dijon mustard
1 whole egg
1 egg yolk
¼ cup fine bread crumbs
2 tablespoons unsalted butter
Tartar Sauce (page 160)

In a large mixing bowl, combine all the ingredients except the butter and the sauce. Form the mixture into cakes, the size depending on whether they are to be used as an appetizer or an entrée.

In a skillet over medium heat, melt the butter and sauté the crab cakes until they are lightly brown, about 2 to 3 minutes per side. Serve with tartar sauce.

Mussels
with Sandía Chile Pasta

Yield: 4 servings

Sandía chiles are a variety of ripe New Mexican red chiles, named for the mountain range outside Albuquerque, the state's largest city. You can use any fresh, pure red chile powder for this recipe. Be sure to avoid commercial chile powder, which contains extraneous ingredients such as salt, sugar, pepper, and cumin. Try to taste chile powder before you buy it, and rub it between your fingers. It should taste hot, a little sweet, and not dusty, and it should stain your fingers a little, showing that the natural oils are still present. For the same reason, good red chile powder should have a slightly lumpy texture and have a fiery, brick-red color.

1 pound Sandía Chile Pasta (recipe follows)
1 teaspoon clarified butter
1/2 teaspoon puréed garlic
1/2 teaspoon puréed shallot
12 mussels, in shells
1/3 cup white wine
Pinch of dried thyme

Pinch of freshly ground black pepper
3/4 cup heavy cream
3 tablespoons grated Asiago cheese
Pinch of salt
Pinch of freshly ground white pepper
1/2 cup chopped fresh cilantro leaves, for garnish

Prepare the pasta, allowing time for it to dry.

To prepare the sauce, melt the butter in a medium skillet and add the garlic purée, shallot purée, mussels, wine, thyme, and black pepper. Cover, and steam the mussels until they open, about 2 or 3 minutes. Shake the pan, remove the mussels, and set them aside. Reserve the cooking liquid.

Cook the pasta *al dente*, drain it, and set it aside.

While the pasta is cooking, reduce the reserved cooking liquid by half and add the cream. Reduce again by half and add the pasta. When the pasta is warm, add the cheese, salt, and white pepper, and reduce again until the sauce thickens. Serve in a soup plate with the pasta on the bottom and the mussels on the half-shell outlining the plate. Garnish with the cilantro.

Sandía Chile Pasta   Yield: about 1 pound; 4 servings

4 large eggs

2 tablespoons pure Sandía or New Mexico red chile powder

1 tablespoon puréed garlic

Salt to taste

2 cups (1 pound) durum flour

Beat the eggs in a stainless steel bowl. In a separate bowl, mix the chile powder with just enough hot water to form a thick paste. Transfer the eggs to a food processor and add the chile paste, garlic purée, and salt. Add the flour and process until the mixture forms a ball. Transfer the dough to a floured board and continue to knead it for 5 minutes. Wrap the dough in plastic and let it rest in the refrigerator for between 15 and 30 minutes.

Roll the dough out in a pasta machine to a thickness of ⅛ inch and let it dry for 10 minutes. Cut the dough into 9- to 12-inch lengths and then cut the sheets into fettucine, about ⅛-inch thick.

Plaza. San Francisco Street at Lincoln Avenue ca. 1866. Courtesy Museum of New Mexico.

Casa Shrimp and Pineapple Curry

Yield: 4 servings

It is interesting that curries, with their spice and heat, originate in hot climates — the Indian subcontinent and Southeast Asia. The theory goes that *picante* foods cause the body to sweat, resulting in a cooling effect — natural air-conditioning, if you will. The climate in the American Southwest is usually warm and dry, so this recipe works equally well here. The tropical tones of the curry spices and pineapple work very well with seafood such as shrimp.

2 tablespoons olive oil
1 onion, finely chopped
1 tablespoon tomato paste
2 tablespoons curry powder
$^1/_2$ cup white wine
1 cup fish stock or clam juice
$1^1/_2$ cups heavy cream

Salt and freshly ground white
   pepper to taste
1 pound shrimp, peeled
   and deveined
1 small pineapple, peeled, cored,
   and diced
Spanish Rice (page 169),
   for serving

Heat the oil in a large skillet and sauté the onion over medium heat for 4 or 5 minutes or until it is translucent. Stir in the tomato paste and curry powder, and increase the heat to medium-high. Add the wine, bring the mixture to a boil, and reduce it slightly. Add the stock or clam juice and reduce the liquid by about one-half.

Lower the heat to medium, add the cream, and let the mixture simmer for between 15 and 20 minutes, until the sauce has thickened. Season with salt and pepper. Add the shrimp and pineapple, and cook until heated through. Serve with the rice.

Poultry & Fowl

*T*he Chinese were the first to raise poultry for food, and the practice was carried to Greece and Rome by way of ancient Asian cultures. Poultry farming has become increasingly important over the past thirty years or so, and is now a major industry as poultry has become the most popular type of meat available, especially in the United States. There is a great variety of poultry available, and all of it fares well with a myriad cooking methods, sauces, and accompaniments, so it is little wonder that it has become a staple in the diet of most countries.

Chicken is the most common and versatile poultry and it's certainly a bonus that the beneficial polyunsaturated omega-3 fats have recently been discovered in their skin. Those of us watching our cholesterol levels can now eat chicken skin without guilt. Poultry and fowl are a good source of protein and minerals such as calcium, iron, phosphorous, riboflavin, niacin, and thiamin.

Turkey is native to the Americas and, when Cortez took the birds back to Europe, they quickly became popular. Because turkey was an important element in the diet of the first settlers in New England, it has become the prerequisite for celebrating the holidays in the United States. More than one politician has suggested that the turkey would be a much more appropriate (as well as peaceloving) emblem for the United States than the predatory eagle is. Definitely better eating.

Quail, duck, and pheasant are also readily available from farm-raised sources as well as in the wild, and they add flamboyance and interest to any menu. They are just as easy to cook as the more predictable chicken and turkey. We recommend that you buy free-range, hormone- and additive-free poultry whenever possible, for flavor as well as health reasons. Next time you think of chicken for your shopping list, be innovative and substitute a different type of bird instead.

La Casa Sena dining room as it appears today.

127

Pollo de Vargas
Grilled Marinated Chicken with Peach and Green Chile Salsa

Yield: 4 servings

This spicy dish is named after Don Diego de Vargas, in these parts a great hero among those descended from the Spanish. He was a general in the Spanish army (based in Mexico) and in 1683 reconquered Santa Fe after it had fallen to the Indians in the Pueblo Revolt. This event is still commemorated in the city in early September with Las Fiestas. Although this doesn't detract from the fun one bit, most of the celebrants haven't the least idea what they're whooping and hollering about, which is probably just as well, given the multiethnic population of Santa Fe today.

2 chickens, 2½ to 3 pounds each, halved lengthwise, wings removed and reserved for another use
1 tablespoon ground cumin

1¼ cups fresh orange juice
¼ cup olive oil
1 tablespoon pure chile powder

Peach and Green Chile Salsa
Yield: about 3 cups

2 small poblano or medium New Mexico green chiles, roasted (page 163), seeded, and chopped
2 tablespoons pure red chile powder

1 cup honey
1 cup chicken stock
2 peaches, peeled, pitted, and chopped
1 teaspoon minced garlic

In a small bowl, whisk together the cumin, orange juice, oil, and 1 tablespoon of the chile powder. Arrange the pieces of chicken in a large shallow baking dish and pour the marinade over them, turning to coat them well. Let the chicken marinate, covered and refrigerated, for at least 1 hour and preferably overnight.

Prepare the grill. While it is heating, make the salsa. In a saucepan, combine the roasted chiles, the 2 tablespoons chile powder, honey, stock, peaches, and garlic. Bring the mixture to a boil, reduce the heat, and simmer for 30 minutes, stirring occasionally, or until the salsa thickens slightly.

Grill the chicken for between 20 and 25 minutes or until it is just cooked through, turning it occasionally and basting it with the marinade. Serve the chicken with the salsa.

Chicken Fajitas

Yield: 4 servings

Fajitas originated in the San Antonio region of Texas, and not, as most people think, in Mexico. They are a relatively recent invention, and were hardly heard of before the 1980s. The word *fajitas* literally means "skirts," a reference to the skirt steak that is traditionally used for beef fajitas. In the Southwest it is common to find both beef and chicken fajitas, and even vegetarian fajitas made with eggplant. Serve fajitas of whatever origin with tortillas, guacamole, salsa, sour cream, and anything else you can find in the fridge.

2 tablespoons olive oil
4 boneless, skinless chicken half breasts, about 4 to 5 ounces each, sliced into strips
1 red bell pepper, seeded and sliced into strips
1 green bell pepper, seeded and sliced into strips
1 red onion, thinly sliced
3 cloves garlic, minced

1 jalapeño chile, seeded and finely diced
1 zucchini, sliced into thin strips
Salt and freshly ground black pepper
8 Whole Wheat Tortillas (page 38)
Guacamole (page 52)
Red Onion Salsa (page 52)
1 cup sour cream

Heat the oil in a large cast-iron skillet. Sauté the chicken over medium-high heat for 4 or 5 minutes. Add the bell peppers, onion, garlic, and *jalapeño*, and sauté for 5 minutes. Add the zucchini and cook for 2 minutes longer. Season with salt and pepper.

Serve the fajitas on a large platter, with warm tortillas, guacamole, salsa, and sour cream on separate plates or bowls. The diners should assemble their own plates by placing some of the fajitas in a tortilla, rolling it, and garnishing to taste with the guacamole, salsa, and sour cream.

Breast of Chicken Eugenie
on Blue Corn Croûtes with Goat Cheese Sauce

Yield: 4 servings

This recipe has its origins in the cuisine of Escoffier, and we think he would have approved of our Santa Fe adaptation using blue corn, Spanish (or Italian) ham, and local goat cheese. Goat cheese is becoming increasingly popular, with good reason, and there are some wonderful Southwestern goat cheeses now being made. As the ingredient list indicates, however, French goat cheese can of course be used, and would make Escoffier himself feel (almost) at home.

4 blue corn croûtes (use the Blue Corn Muffin recipe, page 39)
8 tablespoons unsalted butter
4 large boneless, skinless chicken half breasts
¼ teaspoon freshly ground white pepper
¼ teaspoon fresh lemon juice
4 large mushroom caps
4 slices prosciutto
Goat Cheese Sauce (recipe follows)

To make the blue corn croûtes, follow the recipe for blue corn muffins, but pour the batter into a well-greased cake or cornbread pan. When baked, cut out two 4-inch rounds of blue cornbread and then cut each in half horizontally so you have 4 thin rounds.

Preheat the oven to 350°F.

To cook the chicken, heat 6 tablespoons of the butter in an oven-proof dish and sauté the chicken breasts on the top of the stove for about 1 minute on each side over medium-high heat, until they turn white. Add the pepper and lemon juice, cover tightly, and cook them in the oven for between 6 and 8 minutes.

To cook the mushrooms, heat the remaining 2 tablespoons of butter in a skillet and sauté the mushroom caps gently.

To assemble the rounds, place the cornbread croûtes on serving plates. Heat the prosciutto under the broiler or on a grill and place it on top of the corn bread. Place the chicken breasts on top of the ham and top each serving with ¼ cup of goat cheese sauce and a mushroom cap. Serve the remaining sauce on the side.

Goat Cheese Sauce   Yield: 1¼ cups

1 cup heavy cream

*6 ounces (³⁄₄ cup) goat cheese
   (we use New Mexican
   Coonridge goat cheese)*

1 tablespoon minced garlic

Salt to taste

*Pinch of freshly ground
   white pepper*

In a heavy pan, bring the cream to a boil. Whisk in the goat cheese and minced garlic. When the ingredients are blended, season with salt and pepper.

Piñon-Breaded Chicken
with Mulato Chile and Lingonberry Sauce

Yield: 4 servings

Piñones, or pine nuts, are a significant crop in the Southwest during the fall, and our variety is different from those grown in countries such as Italy and China, or across North Africa. Piñones make a good breading ingredient for meat, and the technique of breading gives an unusual texture.

Mulato chiles are dried *poblanos*, a deep brown in color and relatively mild. Their naturally smoky flavor with overtones of dried fruit makes a perfect match for the rather tart lingonberries, which are related to cranberries.

Mulato Chile and Lingonberry Sauce   Yield: about 3 cups

¼ cup olive oil
2 tablespoons minced garlic
3 tablespoons minced shallots
1 cup Madeira wine
3 dried mulato chiles, rehydrated, seeded, deveined, and finely diced

½ cup bread crumbs
¾ cup pinoñes (pine nuts), coarsely chopped
½ bunch parsley, chopped
½ cup whole wheat flour

3 tablespoons fresh mixed herbs such as basil, oregano, and thyme
2 cups chicken stock
½ cup sugar
1 cup lingonberries in syrup or lingonberry preserves

4 whole, free-range, boneless, skinless chicken breasts, each cut in half
6 egg whites, stirred together until they have liquefied
½ cup olive oil
4 red jalapeño chiles, for garnish

To prepare the sauce, heat the olive oil in a saucepan and sauté the garlic and shallots over medium heat until they begin to brown, about 3 minutes. Add the Madeira and chiles and cook over high heat until the liquid is reduced by half. Add the herbs and stock and continue to cook over high heat until the sauce thickens. Stir in the sugar until it has dissolved, and then add the lingonberries.

Mix the bread crumbs, pine nuts, and parsley together in a mixing bowl. Lightly flour the chicken breasts, dip them into the egg whites, and then into the bread crumb mixture. Heat the olive oil in a skillet and sauté the breaded chicken for 5 minutes on each side until it is cooked through.

Place the sauce on serving plates and serve the chicken on top. Garnish with a fresh red *jalapeño* and serve with steamed baby zucchini.

Grilled Chicken Breast
with Chipotle Chantilly

Yield: 4 servings

This is another delicious recipe that can be adapted to other types of poultry. It's also a recipe that gives a Southwestern twist to a classic presentation. Chantilly is a town in France that has lent its name to dishes featuring whipped cream that is sometimes sweetened (Chantilly has also given its name to a type of lace). The *chipotle* chiles (smoked, dried *jalapeños*) give the cream sauce a marked piquancy as well as a deliciously smoky flavor.

2 tablespoons ground cumin
Juice of 3 oranges
¼ cup olive oil

½ teaspoon salt
8 boneless, skinless chicken half breasts

Chipotle Chantilly   Yield: about 3½ cups

8 egg yolks
Juice of 1 lemon
Pinch of salt
¼ cup water
2 cups melted butter

2 canned chipotle chiles en adobo, seeded and finely minced
1 cup heavy cream, whipped to soft peaks

Mix together the cumin, orange juice, olive oil, and salt in a glass or ceramic bowl and marinate the chicken overnight.

Prepare the grill. While it is heating, prepare the Chipotle Chantilly. Whip the yolks with the lemon, salt, and water in a double boiler set over simmering water. Slowly add the butter in a steady stream while continuing to whip. Whisk in the chiles and fold in the whipped cream. Keep the sauce warm.

Remove the chicken breasts from the marinade and grill them for between 6 and 8 minutes or until the meat springs back when pressed with your finger. Serve with the Chipotle Chantilly.

Roast Turkey
with Mushroom and Herb Stuffing

Yield: 8 to 10 servings

I think everyone in the United States associates turkey with Thanksgiving. By the time Thanksgiving comes along in Santa Fe, we've often had the first snows of winter, although not enough to accumulate to any extent. Less than twenty miles away at the marvelous Santa Fe ski area, several feet will have fallen and the runs are usually already open. There are six other major ski areas within a ninety-minute drive of Santa Fe: Taos, Sandía Peak, Red River, Sipapu, Pajarito, and Angel Fire. Imagine skiing down these powdery slopes as you cook your turkey dinner from the following recipe.

If you have leftovers, consider turkey enchiladas. The recipe is on page 25.

1 uncut loaf (at least 1 day old), trimmed of crust and cut into ½-inch cubes

1 cup (2 sticks) plus 2 tablespoons unsalted butter, diced

2 tablespoons olive oil

10 ounces various wild mushrooms or domestic mushrooms or a mixture, cleaned and sliced

3 shallots, finely chopped

2 tablespoons chopped fresh mixed herbs, such as parsley, thyme, oregano, sage, and rosemary

Salt and freshly ground pepper to taste

1 cup sherry

1 turkey, about 12 to 14 pounds

1 lemon, cut in half

2 cups chicken stock

1 cup heavy cream

Preheat the oven to 350°F.

Place the bread with the one cup of butter on a baking sheet and bake in the oven, turning occasionally, until the cubes are golden brown, about 8 to 10 minutes.

Meanwhile, heat the oil and the remaining 2 tablespoons butter together in a skillet or pan, and sauté the mushrooms over high heat for 2 or 3 minutes. Add the shallots and mixed herbs, and season with salt and pepper. Sauté for another 3 or 4 minutes.

Transfer the bread cubes and the mushrooms to a large mixing bowl, combine thoroughly, and sprinkle the sherry over the mixture.

Rub the turkey cavity and the outside with the lemon, and brush with a little melted butter. Stuff the turkey with the mushroom and herb stuffing. Cover the breast and legs loosely with foil.

Heat the chicken stock in a pan and keep it warm over low heat to use for basting the turkey periodically. Roast the bird in the oven for about 3 or 4 hours, until a meat thermometer inserted at the base of the thigh reads 185 °F.

When the turkey has cooked, let it rest for 15 or 20 minutes before carving it. Strain off the cooking juices and add an equal amount of water. Whisk together and strain, add the cream, and cook the mixture over low heat to make a gravy.

A view of Sena Plaza Courtyard in the '70s with the fountain in the foreground and the old well in the background.

Honey and Chile Roasted Duck
with Raspberry Mole Sauce

Yield: 4 servings

With any type of honey-roasted poultry, the skin is the best part. Chinese emperors are said to have eaten only the honeyed skin of the famous Peking Duck, giving the meat to the servants. The accompanying fruit mole sauce is an adaptation of the classic Mexican *mole poblano*, a sauce made with chiles and chocolate, among many other ingredients. It is the perfect accompaniment for turkey, chicken, or duck.

2 ducks, about 3½ pounds each
Salt and freshly ground
*   black pepper*
8 tablespoons (1 stick)
*   unsalted butter*
6 tablespoons honey

1 tablespoon chile caribe (dried red
*   chile flakes)*
Raspberry Mole Sauce
*   (recipe follows)*
Spanish Rice (page 169),
*   for serving*

Preheat the oven to 425°F.

Season the cavities of the ducks with salt and pepper. Rub the ducks with the butter and place them in a large, ovenproof dish. Brush on (or pour over) the honey, and sprinkle the chile caribe over the honey.

Roast the ducks in the oven for between 30 and 40 minutes or until the juices run clear when the ducks are pierced with a fork or skewer. Remove them from the oven, and let rest for 10 or 15 minutes before carving them. Place the duck slices over the sauce and serve with the rice.

Raspberry Mole Sauce Yield: about 2½ cups

1 tablespoon vegetable oil
1 small carrot, chopped
1 small onion, chopped
1 stalk celery, chopped
1 tomato, chopped
1 small canned chipotle chile en
  adobo, seeded and chopped

1 ounce dark chocolate
¼ cup raspberry vinegar
1½ cups red wine
1 cup beef stock
Salt and freshly ground pepper
  to taste

Heat the oil in a saucepan with a heavy bottom and sauté the carrot, onion, celery, tomato, and *chipotle* over medium heat for 5 to 10 minutes, or until soft. Add the chocolate and cook until it is melted. Add the vinegar and reduce the mixture by half. Add the wine and reduce again by half. Add the stock and reduce again by one half. Together the three reductions will take about 15 minutes.

Remove the sauce from the heat, let it rest for 10 minutes, and then strain it through a fine sieve. Season with salt and pepper.

Roast Pheasant
with Redcurrant Sauce

Yield: 4 servings

Fresh pheasant is ideal for this recipe, but it is hard to come by, and most commercial pheasant comes frozen. In any event, pheasant is tricky to cook, as it can be a little tough and stringy. It's important to baste it often while it is roasting to minimize the risk of its drying out. Young birds (and female pheasants) tend to be juicier and more tender than older or male birds. There must be a moral here somewhere, but whatever it is, it's probably also politically incorrect. You can substitute chicken for the pheasant, although the flavors will obviously be different.

2 pheasant, about 3¹⁄₂ pounds each
2 tablespoons clarified butter
Salt and freshly ground pepper to taste
2 cups beef stock
¹⁄₄ cup crème de cassis liqueur
¹⁄₄ cup fresh redcurrants

Preheat the oven to 450°F.

Brush the pheasant with the butter, and season with salt and pepper. Place them in a roasting pan and roast them in the oven for 10 minutes. Reduce the heat to 350°F and roast for another 40 to 45 minutes, basting frequently with the juices or more clarified butter. When the birds are cooked, the juices will run clear when the thigh is pierced with a skewer or fork. Transfer the pheasant to a serving platter and let them rest for between 5 and 10 minutes.

Meanwhile, in a saucepan, bring the beef stock and cassis to a boil and reduce by half. Add the redcurrants and season with salt and pepper. Serve with the pheasant.

Opposite page:
Grilled Shiitake
Mushrooms, page 61,
and Mini Pizza with
Wild Boar Sausage,
page 62.

Buffalo & Deer Dance
Povi-tan

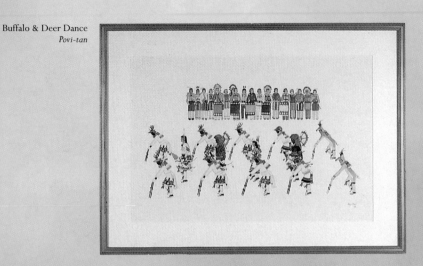

Hunchback Flute Player
Robert Montoya

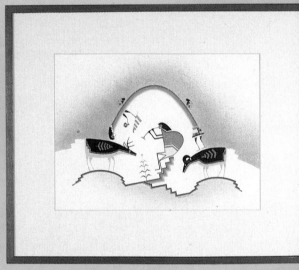

Indian Dancer
Mootska

Roast Quail
with Chipotles and Grapes

Yield: 4 servings

Bobwhite quail are quite common in parts of the Southwest, and quail are also raised commercially, so these days they are widely available. Of course, hunters will tell you that there's nothing quite like range-caught quail. Groups of quail are called bevys, and Easterners and Midwesterners accustomed to hunting large bevys in flat grasslands are usually quite put off by the hard work of stalking their quarry while scrambling over the rocks and through the cactus and tumbleweeds that are part of the Southwestern landscape. Even if your quail is store-bought, you can still tell your guests about the rocks, and cactus, and tumbleweeds for a little additional color!

8 quail
8 tablespoons (1 stick)
*   unsalted butter*
Salt and freshly ground
*   black pepper*
1 cup Port
2 tablespoons tomato paste

2 canned chipotle chiles en adobo
*   (or 2 rehydrated chipotles, see*
*   page 163), seeded and finely*
*   chopped*
1 cup chicken stock
2½ cups (8 to 10 ounces) seedless
*   red grapes*

Preheat the oven to 350°F.

Rub the quail with the butter and season with the salt and pepper. Place them in an ovenproof pan and roast them in the oven for 15 to 20 minutes, basting occasionally. Remove the quail from the oven and keep them warm. Discard the fat in the roasting pan and deglaze it with the Port. Add the tomato paste and reduce the liquid by half. Add the chipotles and chicken stock, and reduce the liquid by two-thirds. Add the grapes and when they are warm, serve the sauce with the quail.

Roast Squab
with Couscous and Red Chile Sauce

Yield: 4 servings

Squab is another name for young, farm-raised pigeon. It has a rich, dark meat and a delicate flavor. It is perfectly matched by the *couscous*, a North African staple made from semolina, and the red chile sauce.

2 tablespoons canola oil
2 tablespoons unsalted butter
4 squab, about 12 ounces each
Salt and freshly ground pepper to taste
5 cups water or chicken stock
4 cups couscous
1 tablespoon finely chopped carrot
1 tablespoon finely chopped shallot

1 clove garlic, finely chopped
1 tablespoon finely chopped fresh basil
1 tablespoon finely chopped fresh parsley
¹/₂ cup Red Chile Sauce (page 159)
2 cups white wine
2 cups beef stock

Preheat the oven to 425°F.

Place the oil and butter in a roasting pan and heat the mixture on the top of the stove until the butter melts. Season the squab with salt and pepper and sauté them in the roasting pan, breast-side down, over high heat for 3 minutes. Transfer the pan to the oven and roast the squab for between 9 and 10 minutes.

Meanwhile, in a large pan, bring the water or stock to a boil (add salt if using water). Add the couscous, carrot, shallot, garlic, and herbs, and cook for 2 minutes. Remove the pan from the heat and let the couscous swell for 5 minutes. Stir with a fork to separate the grains.

In a separate saucepan, combine the red chile sauce and wine and reduce by half over high heat. Add the stock and reduce the liquid by half again — about 20 minutes all told.

Serve the squab with the couscous and the sauce.

Meat & Game

When man was a hunter and gatherer, before becoming agrarian, meat probably constituted the largest part of his diet. Game of all kinds has long been abundant in the American Southwest, but the greatest source of meat before the Europeans arrived on the continent was the buffalo, most of which roamed the Great Plains. The Plains Indians not only ate the meat of the buffalo but also used the hides for clothing and shelter and the bones as utensils.

It has been estimated that there were 30 million of these one-ton animals when the Europeans arrived; only five hundred were left by 1900. Fortunately, this number has increased greatly now that buffalo are being raised both commercially and in preserves. Some Pueblo Indians in New Mexico still perform the colorful Buffalo Dance to honor the creature that played such an important role in their lives. Although we have not included any recipes for buffalo, it can be used in any of the recipes for beef. Buffalo lacks sufficient marbled fat for just plain grilling, but it is good for all other styles of cooking.

Beef remains the most popular meat in the United States and because of this demand we raise the best beef in the world in this country. The better cuts constitute, however, a very small percentage of the animal. To get the prized tenderloins and New York strips that are so important to the menus of fine restaurants all across the country, tons of hamburger must be raised. Hamburger is fine in small doses, but even the leanest burger meat is too high in fat to be consumed as often as it is by so many, especially youngsters.

I can't write about hamburgers without recalling the opening of the Caribbean Beach Club on the island of Antigua in 1960. At the time, there were no hotels of any importance on the island, the roads were primitive, and amenities we now take for granted, such as restaurants and indoor plumbing, were rare or nonexistent. On the second day of training I was eating alone and wrote down my dinner order so as to give the waiter and the kitchen time to plan. I wrote:

1. *Onion soup*
2. *Hamburger*
3. *Chocolate ice cream*
4. *Coffee*

Out came the soup in record time. This was going to be easy! Then out came two hamburgers, and I stopped the waiter before the kitchen could send out three chocolate ice creams and four coffees. Still, this was an improvement on the first day: then I had ordered the same thing verbally and got the ice cream first because "it was the only thing ready."

But, I digress. In the old days, the FDA classifications of Prime and Choice were reliable guides when buying meat; but now we must depend on the supplier. My advice is to find yourselves good butchers and stay with them.

Grilled New York Steak
with Potato and Jalapeño Galettes
and a Red Chile Béarnaise

Yield: 4 servings

The tender cut of beef from the short loin is also known as New York strip steak, shell steak and, in the Midwest, Kansas City steak. The classic French Béarnaise sauce has been given a Southwestern twist with the addition of red chile. Béarnaise was named after the birthplace of the French king, Henry IV — Béarn, in the Basque province. This recipe and our adaptation is appropriate: some of the original Spanish settlers of Santa Fe came from the Basque region.

Red Chile Béarnaise   Yield: about 1½ cups

1 cup white wine
2 tablespoons Red Chile Sauce
*   (page 159)*
½ teaspoon ground cumin
2 tablespoons chopped shallots

1 teaspoon chopped fresh oregano
1 teaspoon chopped fresh cilantro
1 cup clarified butter
3 egg yolks

4 dry-aged New York steaks,
*   about 7 ounces each*
Potato and Jalapeño Galettes
*   (page 170)*

Salt and freshly ground black
*   pepper to taste*

Prepare the grill.

While it is heating, prepare the Béarnaise sauce. Heat the wine, red chile sauce, cumin, and shallots in a saucepan and reduce the mixture to a syrup. Add the herbs and set the mixture aside. Warm the butter in a saucepan over low heat. In a double boiler or over a water bath, beat the egg yolks until they start to thicken, about 2 or 3 minutes. Remove the eggs from the heat and gradually whisk in the warmed butter, in droplets at first. Continue to add the butter and whisk until the sauce thickens to just below boiling. Take care not to let the mixture boil. Add the red chile mixture to the sauce and keep warm.

Season the steaks with salt and pepper and, over high heat, grill the steaks to the desired doneness, about 4 minutes per side for medium rare. Serve the sauce half on the steaks and half to the side, and accompany them with the potato *galettes*.

Sautéed Sirloin Steak
with Ratatouille and Red Wine and Shallot Sauce

Yield: 4 servings

Sirloin steak, like New York strip steak, should be chosen for its cover, marble, and texture. *Cover* refers to the fat around the steak and indicates the length of time the animal was fed grain and, therefore, its tenderness. (You will probably want to trim the cover off before cooking the meat.) The more fat that is marbled through the meat the tastier the steak will be. The texture should be firm but velvety to the touch.

Ratatouille (page 117)
Red Wine and Shallot Sauce (page 109)
2 tablespoons unsalted butter
2 tablespoons canola oil

4 sirloin steaks, about 7 ounces each
Salt and freshly ground black pepper to taste

Prepare the ratatouille and the red wine and shallot sauce.

Heat a sauté pan or cast-iron skillet and add 1 tablespoon each of the butter and oil. Season the steaks with salt and pepper. Place 2 steaks in the pan and, over high heat, sauté them to the desired doneness, about 4 minutes per side for medium rare. Repeat for the remaining 2 steaks. Serve with the ratatouille and red wine and shallot sauce.

Chipotle-Braised Beef

Yield: 8 to 10 servings

Braising meats involves a quick searing followed by lengthy cooking in a tightly sealed container over low heat. This technique makes the meat more tender by gradually breaking down its fiber, so it is one of the best ways to cook the less expensive cuts of meat. The *chipotle* chiles give a flavorful, smoky dimension to this dish, as well as heat. You may use either the canned or dried versions. If they are dried, you will first need to rehydrate them (see page 163).

*1 recipe Chipotle Marinade for
  Beef (page 166)
6 pounds beef — chuck, rump,
  top round, or sirloin —
  trimmed and tied*

*Salt and freshly ground black
  pepper to taste
¼ cup olive oil
6 cups beef stock*

Make up the marinade and use it to marinate the beef overnight in a glass or ceramic container in the refrigerator.

The next day, preheat the oven to 350°F.

Drain the meat, reserving the marinade, and pat dry with paper towels. Season it with salt and pepper. In a casserole or ovenproof dish large enough to hold the meat, heat the oil on top of the stove, add the meat, and quickly sear it on all sides over high heat. Add the marinade and reduce the liquid by half. Add the stock, bring it to a boil, cover the dish, and braise the meat in the oven for between 2 and 2½ hours. Turn the meat 2 or 3 times while it is cooking.

Transfer the meat to a serving platter, and cover it loosely with foil. Strain the cooking juices into a saucepan, skim off the fat, and reduce the liquid to 2 or 3 cups. Season with salt and pepper and pour into a gravy boat.

Carve the meat at the table and pass the sauce separately.

Marinated Pork Chops
with Braised Spicy Red Cabbage

Yield: 4 servings

The pork and cabbage in this recipe make marvelous partners. Cabbage is one of the oldest cultivated vegetables, and was introduced to North America by the early European settlers; the word itself is originally derived from the French *caboche*, meaning head. The influx of German immigrants in the mid-1800s boosted the popularity of cabbage, and the sizable community they established around New Braunfels in Texas probably marked the dawn of the era of cabbage growing in the Southwest. It seems fitting then that we have combined cabbage with *jalapeño* chiles, which are also grown widely in the Lone Star State.

1 recipe Jalapeño Marinade for Pork (page 166)

4 pork chops, about 6 to 8 ounces each

1 tablespoon canola oil

Braised Spicy Red Cabbage

1 head red cabbage, thinly sliced

1 onion, diced

4 apples, cored, peeled, halved, and thinly sliced

2 jalapeño chiles, seeded and finely diced

3 cloves

2 tablespoons sugar

2 tablespoons red wine vinegar

1 cup red wine

Salt and freshly ground black pepper to taste

Make up the marinade in a glass or ceramic bowl; add the pork chops and let them marinate for at least 3 hours in the refrigerator.

Meanwhile, prepare the cabbage. Place the cabbage, onion, apples, jalapeños, cloves, sugar, vinegar, wine and salt and pepper in a heavy-bottomed pan, bring the mixture to a boil, and simmer it slowly, covered, for between 45 and 50 minutes. Add more wine if necessary and season with salt and pepper.

Preheat the oven to 375°F.

Remove the chops from the marinade, and reserve the marinade. Heat the canola oil in a large pan or skillet and brown the chops for 3 minutes on each side. Transfer the chops to a casserole or ovenproof dish and baste them generously with the reserved marinade. Cook the chops in the oven for between 20 and 25 minutes, turning and basting them once or twice. Serve the chops with the braised cabbage.

Grilled Marinated Pork Tenderloin
with Papaya and Chipotle Chutney

Yield: 4 servings

These days, pork is much leaner than it ever used to be. In fact, pork tenderloin, because of its relatively low fat content, has even been served at
some recent functions of the American Heart Association in Santa Fe.
I think pork tenderloin is one of the best and most overlooked pieces of
meat, but it must be cooked perfectly: too little and most diners are
repelled by the risk of trichinosis; too much, and it turns out dry. The
best way to get it just right is to insert a meat thermometer and cook it
to medium (about 165 °F).

*1 recipe Jalapeño Marinade for
    Pork (page 166)*
*4 pork tenderloins, about 8 ounces
    each, trimmed of fat*

*Papaya and Chipotle Chutney
    (recipe follows)*

Make up the marinade, add the pork, and let it marinate for at least 3 hours
in the refrigerator.

Prepare the papaya and chipotle chutney, allowing time for it to cool
to room temperature and then chill in the refrigerator.

Remove the tenderloins from the marinade, and reserve the marinade.
Grill or broil the tenderloins over medium-high heat for 7 or 8 minutes per
side, turning occasionally and basting them with the marinade. Slice the pork
into medallions, and arrange them in a fan on serving plates. Spoon the chutney over the pork to half cover each medallion.

Papaya and Chipotle Chutney   Yield: about 4 cups

*4 papayas, seeded, peeled, and cut
into ⅛-inch dice*

*1 small yellow onion, finely
chopped*

*2 apples, peeled, cored, and cut
into ⅛-inch dice*

½ cup sugar

¼ cup raspberry vinegar

*2 dried chipotle chiles, rehydrated
(see page 163) and finely
chopped (or 2 chipotle chiles en
adobo sauce)*

½ cup water

In a heavy-bottomed saucepan, combine half of the papaya with all of the
remaining ingredients. Bring the mixture to a boil, stirring the ingredients together. Reduce the heat and simmer the chutney slowly for
1 hour, stirring occasionally.

Remove the saucepan from the heat and stir in the remaining papaya.
Allow the mixture to cool for 1 hour at room temperature before refrigerating it. Serve cold.

Sena Plaza in the '40s showing the earliest stages of the now lush garden.

Grilled Pork Tenderloin
with Broccoli Raab and Corn and Garlic Salsa

Yield: 4 servings

Broccoli raab is not in fact a type of broccoli but a green vegetable related to the cabbage and turnip. It's better known as rape, especially in Europe, and is the same plant that produces rapeseed or canola oil. The leaves are tasty and a little pungent. You can substitute other greens if broccoli raab is unavailable.

It is important in this recipe, as in all the others, to use fresh garlic; never use powdered garlic or garlic salt.

1 recipe Cilantro Marinade for Pork (page 166)
4 pork tenderloins, about 8 ounces each, trimmed of fat
Roasted Corn and Garlic Salsa (recipe follows)

1 tablespoon olive oil
2 cloves garlic, finely chopped
1 pound broccoli raab
Salt and freshly ground black pepper to taste

Make up the marinade in a glass or ceramic dish, add the pork tenderloins, and let them marinate for at least 3 hours in the refrigerator.

Meanwhile, make the salsa and prepare the grill.

Remove the tenderloins from the marinade, and reserve the marinade. Grill the tenderloins over medium-high heat (or alternatively, broil them) for between 7 and 8 minutes per side, turning occasionally, and basting them with the marinade. Slice the pork into medallions.

Heat the olive oil in a saucepan and sauté the garlic over medium-high heat for 1 minute. Add the broccoli raab and sauté for 3 or 4 more minutes. Carefully add 2 tablespoons of water to the pan to "steam" the broccoli raab. Season with salt and pepper.

Serve the pork over the broccoli raab, and spoon the salsa on one side of the plate.

Roasted Corn and Garlic Salsa   Yield: about 1½ cups

2 small ears corn
⅓ cup plus 1 teaspoon olive oil
Salt and freshly ground pepper to taste
6 cloves garlic
2 tablespoons raspberry vinegar

1 serrano or ½ jalapeño chile, seeded and finely chopped
1 teaspoon chopped fresh parsley
1 teaspoon diced red bell pepper
½ shallot, minced

Preheat the oven to 350°F.

Remove the husks and silk from the corn and drizzle 1 teaspoon of the olive oil over the kernels. Season them with salt and pepper and wrap the ears, together with the garlic, in foil. Roast them in the oven for between 40 and 45 minutes. Remove the package from the oven, cut the kernels from the cobs (this should yield about ¾ cup), and chop the garlic finely.

Meanwhile, combine the remaining ⅓ cup olive oil and the vinegar, chile, parsley, bell peppers, and shallot in a glass or ceramic bowl. Add the roasted corn and garlic and season to taste.

La Casa Sena's Corona del Cordero

with Basil Pesto, Green Chile Jelly, and Red Chile and Pine Nut Salsa

Yield: 4 servings

Rocky Mountain lamb is the best in the world (let's not mince words or pull punches!) and it thrives in many parts of Colorado and New Mexico. Lamb was originally brought to the American Southwest by the Spanish, who brought their *Churro* sheep with them from Mexico. This breed, also herded by Southwestern native Americans, are also known as Navajo sheep. Although their numbers have dwindled and their relative importance in the sheep population diminished, they are well suited to the terrain. Utah State University recently embarked on a program to expand their numbers.

2 racks of lamb, about 2 to 3 pounds each

Basil Pesto   Yield: about 1¼ cups

*2 cups (about 2 ounces) basil,
   leaves only*
3 cloves garlic, minced
6 sundried tomatoes, rehydrated
¼ cup olive oil
¼ cup toasted piñones (pine nuts)
Salt to taste

Green Chile Jelly   Yield: about 2 cups

*5 roasted New Mexico green chiles
   (page 163), peeled, seeded,
   and finely diced*
¾ cup clover honey
1 teaspoon chopped fresh cilantro
Juice of 1 orange
3 ounces pectin (such as Certo)
Salt to taste

Red Chile and Pine Nut Salsa   Yield: about 1 cup

*1 cup full-bodied red wine, such as
   Cabernet Sauvignon or Chianti*
1 cup beef stock
½ cup heavy cream
1 clove garlic, minced
¼ cup toasted piñones (pine nuts)
½ cup pure red chile powder
Salt to taste

Trim the racks of lamb and set aside.

To prepare the basil *pesto*, purée all the ingredients together in a blender. Cover the racks of lamb with the pesto, and marinate for at least 3 hours, but preferably overnight in the refrigerator.

Preheat the oven to 375°F.

To prepare the green chile jelly, place all the ingredients together in a saucepan, bring them to a boil, and cook for 10 minutes. Let the jelly cool.

To prepare the salsa, place the wine in a saucepan, bring it to a boil, and reduce it by half. Add the stock and reduce by half again. Add the cream, garlic, pine nuts, chile powder, and salt, and reduce the liquid to the consistency of a sauce. This should take about 20 minutes.

Place the lamb in a roasting pan and roast the racks for 10 minutes for rare, 20 minutes for medium rare, or 30 minutes for medium. Let the meat rest for several minutes before carving it.

San Francisco Street at Plaza ca. 1885. Courtesy Museum of New Mexico.

Grilled Marinated Lamb Chops
with Potato Gratin and Peach and Green Chile Salsa

Yield: 4 servings

Fresh American lamb is so good, it's a shame to buy frozen lamb from some distant land. The problem with freezing meat is that it has to be thawed and, however it's done, that ruins the meat. Ideally, lamb should be cooked to medium rare, but of course, personal taste should be the abiding criterion. The separate elements of this dish combine together wonderfully well.

2 recipes Port Marinade for Lamb (page 165)
12 lamb loin chops, about 5 ounces each

Peach and Green Chile Salsa (page 128)
Potato Gratin (page 170)

Make up the marinade, doubling the quantities given in the recipe, add the lamb and let the chops marinate for at least 3 hours, but preferably overnight, in the refrigerator.

Make the salsa and the potato gratin, which needs 40 minutes to cook. Prepare the grill. Remove the lamb chops from the marinade and grill them over medium-high heat to the desired doneness, about 3 or 4 minutes per side for medium rare. Serve with the salsa and potatoes.

Opposite page:
Grilled Venison with
Roasted Corn and
Poblano Chile Relish,
page 156. The bottle of
Pinot Noir shows a label
by Paul Wonner.

Pueblo at Santa Fe
Warren E. Rollins

Pueblo Portrait
Gerald Cassidy

Santa Clara Dancer
Bettina Steinke

Roast Leg of Lamb
with Chile Crust

Yield: 4 servings

Ask your butcher to remove the leg bone and include it in the package so you can roast it with the lamb for its juices. This is a straightforward recipe, and the *picante* crust provides an interesting contrast in texture as well as flavor. As an alternative to the bread crumbs, and for a richer crust, you can use finely chopped nuts, such as pecans.

1 leg of lamb, about 4 to 5 pounds, bone out

1 head of garlic, cut in half horizontally

1 tablespoon unsalted butter

Salt and freshly ground black pepper to taste

1 cup bread crumbs

2 tablespoons pure red chile powder

Preheat the oven to 425°F.

Rub the lamb with one half of the head of garlic. Then rub it with the butter and season with salt and pepper. Place the lamb in a roasting pan together with the garlic and the leg bone (if you have it) and roast the meat in the oven for about 1 hour. Remove the lamb from the oven and let it rest for between 20 and 30 minutes. Discard the bone.

Prepare the broiler.

Blend the bread crumbs and chile powder together. When the lamb is cool, spread the bread crumb mixture over the lamb, and broil it for between 6 and 8 minutes. Serve with boiled red potatoes and a salad.

Grilled Venison
with Roasted Corn and Poblano Chile Relish

Yield: 4 servings

Venison is probably the most healthful meat there is: It's lean and low in fat and cholesterol, as well as being tender and tasty. This recipe is similar to one I ate near the Weiner Wald, except there weren't too many poblano chiles to be found in Austria.

*1 recipe Jalapeño Marinade for
   Pork (page 166)*
*4 venison steaks, about
   8 ounces each*

*Roasted Corn and Poblano Chile
   Relish (recipe follows)*

Make up the marinade in a glass or ceramic bowl, add the venison, and let it marinate for at least 3 hours, or preferably overnight in the refrigerator.

Make the relish, allowing time for it to sit so that the flavors will meld.

Remove the venison from the marinade and grill it over medium-high heat for 3 minutes per side, until just done. Slice and arrange in a fan on serving plates. Spoon the relish over only half of each slice of venison.

Roasted Corn and Poblano Relish   Yield: about 2½ cups

1 ear corn
½ teaspoon vegetable oil
*1 roasted poblano chile
   (page 163), peeled, seeded,
   and diced*
*½ roasted red bell pepper
   (page 163), peeled, seeded,
   and diced*

1 shallot, finely chopped
2 cloves garlic, finely chopped
½ bunch cilantro, chopped
½ cup olive oil
¼ cup sherry vinegar
*Salt and freshly ground black
   pepper to taste*

Preheat the oven to 400°F.

Remove the outer layer of corn husk and pull the inner layers back to expose the kernels. Remove the corn silk, brush the ear with the vegetable oil, and season it lightly with salt. Replace the husks over the kernels, place the ear on a cookie sheet, and roast it in the oven for between 25 and 30 minutes. Let the corn cool and cut the kernels from the cob.

Place the corn, roasted *poblano* and bell pepper, shallot, garlic, cilantro, olive oil, vinegar, salt, and pepper in a mixing bowl, combine well, and let the mixture sit for 2 hours to blend the flavors.

Sauces, Basics, & Marinades

*T*he recipes that follow include the basic building blocks on which many of our dishes rely.

The sauces included here, for instance, may be used as accompanying sauces but, in many recipes, they are themselves ingredients. Other recipes for sauces, salsas, chutneys, and relishes are scattered throughout the text to reflect the ways we use them in the restaurant; we have chosen to supply the recipe for the accompaniment with the recipe for the main dish.

Some of the marinades given here are called for in specific recipes; others we have not used elsewhere. Grilled food is common in Southwestern cuisine and these excellent, all-purpose, any-occasion marinades are the perfect preparation.

All the side dishes, too, will come in handy again and again. In this section, we include recipes for those that we find ourselves using often; recipes for others that are scattered throughout the book reflect, like the recipes for the sauces, the partnerships we have devised for them in the restaurant.

Much of our continuing fascination for food probably comes from the possibilities of combining flavors and textures. Even as you are reading this, we are likely to be discovering new favorite combinations. The index provides a useful place for browsing and letting your imagination spark possibilities of original and interesting combinations.

Red Chile Sauce

Yield: about 5 cups

Red chile sauce is one of the true staples of Southwestern cuisine. Because it is used in a number of recipes, and can be paired with eggs, sausages, enchiladas, tacos, most red meat, and many other foods, it is worth making up a batch of this sauce in the quantity given below and storing it in the refrigerator.

1 tablespoon olive oil
2 cloves garlic, finely chopped
2 shallots, finely chopped
1 tablespoon cornstarch

2 tablespoons pure red chile powder (preferably Chimayó or other New Mexican red chile)
3 cups chicken or vegetable stock
Salt and freshly ground pepper to taste

In a saucepan or large skillet, heat the olive oil and sauté the garlic and shallots over medium heat until they are translucent, about 2 or 3 minutes. Dissolve the cornstarch in ¼ cup of the cold stock, and add it to the pan. (You can use more or less cornstarch, depending on the thickness of sauce you prefer.) Add the red chile. Add the remaining stock and bring the mixture to a boil. Reduce the heat and allow the chile sauce to simmer for between 25 and 30 minutes. Add salt and pepper to taste.

Red Chile Jelly

Yield: about 2 cups

This recipe works just as well with fresh (or frozen) New Mexico green chiles in case you can't find the red or if you just want a green jelly for a change. Simply substitute the same quantity of green chiles and green bell pepper for the red. (For a green chile jelly flavored with honey, see page 152).

1 cup sugar
½ cup cider vinegar
2 to 3 fresh New Mexico red chiles, finely chopped

½ red bell pepper, seeded and finely chopped
2 tablespoons pectin

In a saucepan, combine the sugar, vinegar, chiles, and bell pepper. Bring the mixture to a boil, reduce the heat and simmer for about 5 minutes, stirring until the sugar has completely dissolved. Add the pectin and boil for 1 minute, stirring continuously, until it is completely dissolved. Pour the jelly into a screw-top glass jar and allow it to cool. Keep refrigerated.

Green Chile Sauce

Yield: about 5 cups

Here is the green version of the ubiquitous chile sauce. Some green New Mexico chiles can be much hotter than others, so vary the quantity of chiles according to taste. Most of the state's green chile crop is grown in the Rio Grande valley of southern New Mexico, near Hatch and Las Cruces, and this is where the chile we use comes from.

1 tablespoon olive oil
2 cloves garlic, finely chopped
2 shallots, finely chopped
*1 pound fresh New Mexico green
    chile, roasted (page 163),
    seeded, peeled, and diced*

3 cups chicken or vegetable stock
1 teaspoon chopped fresh oregano
1½ tablespoons cornstarch
2 tablespoons cold water
*Salt and freshly ground pepper
    to taste*

In a skillet, heat the olive oil and sauté the garlic and shallots over medium heat until translucent, about 2 to 3 minutes. Add the green chile, stock, and oregano. Dissolve the cornstarch in the water and add it to the mixture. (You can use more or less cornstarch, depending on the thickness of sauce you prefer.) Bring the mixture to a boil, reduce the heat, and allow the chile sauce to simmer for between 25 and 30 minutes. Add salt and pepper to taste.

Tartar Sauce

Yield: about 1⅓ cups

2 tablespoons chopped cornichons
2 tablespoons chopped capers
1 chopped shallot
1 teaspoon Dijon mustard
*½ cup chopped fresh
    Italian parsley*

½ cup Crème Fraîche (page 161)
*Salt and freshly ground pepper
    to taste*
Paprika to taste

In a small mixing bowl, combine all the ingredients thoroughly.

Mayonnaise

Yield: about 1¾ cups

Of course, it may be more convenient to use store-bought mayonnaise, but it's easy to tell the difference in quality when you make your own. We think it's worth the extra effort.

1 whole egg
2 egg yolks
½ teaspoon salt
¼ teaspoon freshly ground
    black pepper

2 teaspoons fresh lemon juice
1 cup canola oil
½ cup extra virgin olive oil

Place the egg and yolks in a blender or food processor and purée them for 10 seconds. Add the salt, pepper, and lemon juice, and purée for 10 seconds longer. Combine the oils and, with the machine running, gradually add them in a steady stream. Thin the mixture with a little more lemon juice or water if desired. Keep chilled.

Mayonnaise should keep in the refrigerator for 1 week.

Crème Fraîche

Yield: 2 cups

This recipe (or one very similar) is known as crema in Mexico. It is most commonly used with spicy food to cool the palate. It should be prepared at least twelve hours, preferably twenty-four hours, ahead of time.

1 cup sour cream or buttermilk,
    preferably unpasteurized

1 cup heavy cream

In a mixing bowl, whisk the ingredients together. Cover with plastic wrap and let the mixture sit in a warm place for 12 hours. Transfer the crème fraîche to the refrigerator and chill it.

Crème fraîche should keep in the refrigerator for at least 1 week.

Croutons

Yield: about 3 cups

These come in handy for all sorts of uses — soups, salads, or even for snacks. Use bread that's at least a day old. (A recipe for goat-cheese croutons may be found on page 73.)

3 tablespoons unsalted butter
½ cup olive oil
2 cloves garlic, minced (optional)

3 cups bread (preferably French baguette), cut into ¾-inch dice

Preheat the oven to 350°F.

Heat the butter and oil in a large skillet or sauté pan and sauté the garlic over medium-low heat for 2 minutes. Add the bread, tossing it well so that the cubes are coated evenly. Transfer the bread to a cookie sheet and bake the croutons in the oven for between 15 and 20 minutes or until they are lightly browned.

Roasted Corn

Corn may be roasted while it is still on the cob or one can roast the kernels oneself. There is a recipe for roasting the whole cob on page 151; for the kernels on page 76. Use whichever method is convenient; there is very little difference in the results.

Roasted Garlic

A supply of roasted garlic will frequently come in handy. The flavor, which is mellower than that of raw garlic, gives dishes a subtle sweetness.

Peel the cloves from a head of garlic and toss them with 1 tablespoon of oil until they are thoroughly coated. Spread the cloves out on a roasting pan, cover the pan with foil, and cook the garlic in a 350°F, oven for 30 minutes. Remove the foil and return the pan to the oven for 5 minutes longer, to brown the garlic.

Roasted Peppers

Well-roasted chiles and bell peppers should have blackened and blistered skin, but the flesh should not be burned.

Arrange the peppers on a wire rack that has been set over a gas flame and turn them frequently so that the skins are blackened uniformly. (The flame should be hot enough to char the skin without cooking the peppers.) Transfer the peppers to a bowl and cover them with plastic wrap or drop them into a paper bag, seal the top, and set the bag aside. Let the peppers steam in the bowl or bag for about 15 or 20 minutes. When the peppers are cool enough to handle, peel off the paper-thin skin, remove the seeds, and slice, dice, mince or purée the peppers, depending on what you plan to use them for.

Lacking a gas flame, you may roast peppers on a grill or under a broiler or dip them in hot oil (400°F) and keep them there until the skin blisters.

Rehydrated Chiles

Dried chiles may be soaked in warm water to cover for about 30 minutes. Drain and proceed with the recipe. The soaking water may be used to provide some of the liquid in certain dishes. At La Casa Sena we consider that dried and fresh chiles are too dissimilar to be interchangeable.

Roasted Tomatillos

Remove the papery husk and rinse the tomatillos. Dry-roast them in a hot skillet over medium heat for between 10 and 15 minutes, shaking the pan occasionally to roast them evenly. Take care not to let the tomatillos burn.

Court Bouillon

Yield: about 4 cups

1 cup white wine
2 quarts water
1 small carrot, sliced
¹/₂ an onion, chopped

2 bay leaves
¹/₂ lemon
2 stalks celery, sliced
8 black peppercorns

Place all the ingredients in a large saucepan, bring the mixture to a boil, and simmer for 45 minutes. Strain and set aside to cool.

Marinade for Salmon

Yield: about 2 cups, enough for a 1 pound filleted salmon

2 cups olive oil
2 heads garlic, each cut in half
  horizontally

12 sprigs fresh thyme
6 sprigs fresh rosemary
12 black peppercorns, crushed

Combine all the ingredients in a large mixing bowl.

Marinate the fish in the refrigerator for 24 hours, then drain off the marinade and grill the salmon for 4 or 5 minutes a side (this will depend on the thickness) for medium.

Soy Marinade for Fish

Yield: about 1¾ cups; enough for 4 fillets (about 6 ounces each)

1 cup soy sauce
¹/₂ cup sugar

2 tablespoons minced ginger
1 tablespoon minced garlic

Combine all the ingredients in a saucepan, bring the mixture to a boil, remove the pan from the heat, and set the marinade aside to cool before using it.

Fish should be marinated, at room temperature, for between 15 and 20 minutes.

Epazote Marinade for Shrimp

Yield: about ½ cup; enough for 8 ounces small shrimp

2 tablespoons olive oil
1 tablespoon fresh lemon juice
2 cloves garlic, minced

1 shallot minced
1 tablespoon chopped fresh
    epazote

Combine all the ingredients and mix well.

Shrimp should be marinated for about 30 minutes before cooking.

Chile Caribe Marinade for Chicken Breasts

Yield: about ⅔ cup, enough for between 4 and 6 whole chicken breasts

½ cup olive oil
2 tablespoons fresh lime juice
1 teaspoon chile caribe (dried red
    chile flakes)

1 tablespoons chopped fresh
    cilantro
½ teaspoon salt

Combine all the ingredients in a large glass or ceramic bowl.

Port Marinade for Lamb

Yield: about ¾ cup, enough for 6 lamb chops (about 1½ pounds)

½ cup olive oil
¼ cup Port
1 head garlic, cut in half
    horizontally

3 sprigs fresh rosemary
6 black peppercorns, crushed

Combine all the ingredients in a large mixing bowl.

Lamb should be marinated in the refrigerator, for at least 3 hours and, preferably, overnight.

Jalapeño Marinade for Pork

Yield: about 2½ cups; enough for four 8-ounce pork tenderloins or chops

¾ cup sherry vinegar
1½ cups olive oil
1½ teaspoons chopped garlic
1½ teaspoons chopped shallot

3 jalapeño chiles, seeded
  and chopped
¾ teaspoon ground cumin
1½ teaspoons salt

In a glass or ceramic bowl thoroughly combine all the ingredients.

Pork should be marinated for about 3 hours in the refrigerator. This marinade may also be used for venison, which should be marinated, again in the refrigerator, overnight.

Cilantro Marinade for Pork

Yield: about 2¾ cups, enough for four 8-ounce pork tenderloins or chops

2 cups olive oil
½ cup fresh lemon juice
½ cup chopped fresh cilantro
2 tablespoons chopped
  fresh oregano
2 cloves garlic, chopped

1 tablespoon pure red chile powder
1 teaspoon ground cumin
⅛ teaspoon salt
⅛ teaspoon freshly ground
  black pepper

In a glass or ceramic bowl, combine all the ingredients and mix thoroughly.

Pork should be marinated for about 3 hours in the refrigerator.

Chipotle Marinade for Beef

Yield: about 6½ cups; enough for a 6-pound cut of beef

6 cups red wine
3 chipotle chiles, either canned en
  adobo sauce or dried and
  rehydrated (see page 163),
  finely diced
3 cloves garlic, finely diced

3 carrots, thinly sliced
1 tablespoon grated fresh ginger
6 sprigs fresh thyme
1 sprig fresh rosemary
½ bunch fresh parsley, finely
  chopped

Combine all of the ingredients in a glass or ceramic bowl and mix well.

A whole cut of beef should be marinated overnight in the refrigerator.

Side Dishes

Black Beans

To make black beans for a side dish, refer to either of the soup recipes on pages 71 and 72. When the beans are cooked, drain them and reserve the liquid. Use the beans and a little of the liquid. Any remaining beans can be used with the rest of the liquid for soup.

Posole

Yield: about 5 cups

2 pounds prepared blue or yellow posole corn
6 cups water, or enough to cover
1 small onion, finely chopped
2 cloves garlic, minced

1 tablespoon chile caribe (dried red chile flakes)
$^1/_2$ tablespoon dried oregano
1 bay leaf
$^1/_2$ teaspoon salt

Place the posole corn and water in a large saucepan and simmer, covered, for between 2 and 2$^1/_2$ hours until the *posole* is tender. Add more water if necessary, to keep the posole covered. Add the remaining ingredients and simmer for a further 30 minutes. Remove the bay leaf and serve.

Spinach and Cheese Pancakes

Yield: about 8 small pancakes

$^1/_2$ cup milk
1 cup bread crumbs
$^1/_2$ bunch spinach

1 egg
$^2/_3$ cup grated Monterey Jack cheese
2 tablespoons unsalted butter

In a mixing bowl, combine the milk and bread crumbs and set aside for 30 minutes. Meanwhile, blanch the spinach for 1 minute in boiling water, drain, and place it in ice water. Squeeze out the excess water and chop the spinach coarsely.

Squeeze the excess milk from the bread crumbs. Add the chopped spinach, egg, and cheese to the bread crumbs and mix together well. Form into small pancakes, using about 2 tablespoons of the mixture per pancake.

In a nonstick sauté pan or skillet, heat the butter and sauté the pancakes for about 4 to 6 minutes per side. Serve immediately.

Potato Pie

Yield: 6 to 8 servings

This is a simple, delicious, and versatile side dish that can also be served with eggs for breakfast.

2 sheets puff pastry (enough to line and cover a 9-inch pan)
1¼ pounds potatoes, sliced
¼ cup chopped fresh parsley
Salt and freshly ground pepper to taste

6 strips bacon
4 hard-boiled eggs, sliced
1 egg
1 tablespoon water or milk

Preheat the oven to 400°F.

Line the bottom of a 9-inch pie pan with half of the puff pastry. In a mixing bowl, toss the potato slices with the parsley, salt, and pepper. Sauté the bacon in a skillet until it is just cooked. Arrange a layer of potatoes on the pastry lining the bottom of the pie pan adding, in this order, layers of bacon, egg, more bacon, and more potato. Cover with the remaining puff pastry. Press the edges together well to form a seal. Make a small hole in the middle of the pie, and make a chimney with a piece of aluminum foil. Place the chimney firmly into the hole.

Whisk together the egg and water to make a wash and brush it over the top of the pie. Bake in the oven for 20 minutes, then turn the heat down to 350°F and cook for 45 minutes longer. Then reduce the heat to 300°F and bake for 10 minutes.

Spanish Rice

Yield: 6 to 8 servings

¼ cup olive oil
1 cup finely chopped celery
1 yellow onion, finely chopped
2 cups rice
1½ cups water

1 can (28 ounces) coarsely chopped tomatoes (including liquid)
Salt and freshly ground pepper to taste

In a large pan or skillet, heat the olive oil and sauté the celery and onion over medium heat for between 3 and 5 minutes. Add the rice, water, and tomatoes, and bring the mixture to a boil. Reduce the heat to low and simmer, covered tightly, for about 45 minutes, until the rice is tender. Season with salt and pepper to taste.

Potato Gratin

Yield: 6 servings

5 baking potatoes, thinly sliced
2 cups half-and-half
2 cloves garlic, minced
Salt and freshly ground pepper
  to taste

Ground nutmeg to taste
1⅓ cups (4 ounces) grated
  Monterey Jack cheese
3 tablespoons unsalted butter,
  cut into small dice

Preheat the oven to 350°F. Butter a gratin dish or ovenproof dish.

In a heavy-bottomed saucepan, combine the potatoes, half-and-half, garlic, salt, pepper, and nutmeg, and bring the mixture to a boil. Reduce the heat and simmer for 5 minutes. Remove the saucepan from the heat and drain the potatoes, reserving the liquid. Place half of the potatoes in the gratin dish. Sprinkle half of the cheese over the potatoes. Add the remaining potatoes and sprinkle with the butter and remaining cheese. Pour the cooking liquid over the potatoes and cheese so that it just covers them.

Bake the gratin in the oven for between 30 and 40 minutes or until it is browned.

Potato and Jalapeño Galettes

Yield: 12 three-inch galettes

2 cups grated potato
2 jalapeño chiles, seeded and finely
  diced
2 eggs, lightly beaten

Salt and freshly ground pepper
  to taste
4 tablespoons clarified butter

In a large bowl, combine the potato, *jalapeños*, eggs, and salt and pepper. Form the mixture into round *galettes* or cakes about 3 inches in diameter.

Heat a little of the butter in a nonstick pan and sauté each galette for 4 to 5 minutes per side over medium heat, or until it is golden brown.

Once cooked, keep the galettes warm in a low oven while you cook the rest.

Desserts

*A*s anyone who has traveled to Mexico will know, desserts are not a major element of the cuisine. The repertoire of traditional Southwestern cuisine is, likewise, somewhat limited. The recipes in this chapter include, however, some of the standbys of the region, such as flans, *natillas*, and *biscochitos*. Others make use of the soft fruit that is an important agricultural product of the Southwest and indigenous items such as *piñones*. Some of these desserts are classics at La Casa Sena and, if we didn't publish them, we would get a heap of complaint letters.

Gordon Heiss's wife, Kay "Cricket" Heiss, hardly sounds like the registered dietician that she is when she advises people to eat their dessert first. Her rationale is that most people love desserts so much that they will eat it no matter how full they are after a meal. If they eat dessert first, perhaps they will eat fewer calories during the main part of the meal. This iconoclastic idea may never become a general custom, but at least now you have an excuse if you do decide to take it up.

It is widely reported in the restaurant business that serious diners are currently steering away from cream sauces, fried foods, and rich entrées. Perhaps they are. But, when it comes to dessert, there has been a noticeable increase in sales regardless of chocolate, cream, or butter content. It's almost as though people are rewarding their sweet tooth and tastebuds for all the willpower exerted during the first part of the meal. We pitch our tent with this decadent majority!

Chocolate Mousse Torte

Yield: 1 torte; 12 servings

Chocolate desserts will only be as good as the chocolate you use, and there is a vast difference in quality out there, as we've discovered in creating our new Santa Fe Chocolate Company. In a recent taste testing of twenty-seven of the world's best chocolates held at the Chefs' Cuisiniers Club in New York, a group of forty-six international chefs and chocolatiers proclaimed the Valrhona Equatoriale brand to be the winner.

Crust

³/₄ cup unsalted butter, softened
4 cups chocolate wafer crumbs
  (1¹/₂ boxes Famous brand chocolate wafers; about 17 ounces)

Filling

1 pound semisweet chocolate chips   *2 cups heavy cream*
2 whole eggs   *6 tablespoons powdered sugar*
4 eggs, separated

Topping

2 cups heavy cream   *¹/₂ teaspoon vanilla extract*
¹/₄ cup sugar

To prepare the crust, mix the butter with the crumbs in a mixing bowl until they mass together. Press the "dough" into a 9-inch springform pan and chill it in the refrigerator for at least 30 minutes.

To prepare the filling, melt the chocolate chips in a double boiler and allow them to cool until the chocolate is lukewarm (about 95°F). Beat in the whole eggs and egg yolks. In a mixing bowl, whip the cream with the powdered sugar until soft peaks form. In a separate bowl, whisk the egg whites until they are stiff but not dry. Stir some of the whipped cream and some of the whipped egg white into the chocolate mixture to lighten it. Then, by hand, fold in the rest of the whipped cream and egg white. Pour the filling into the prepared crust and chill the tart for 6 hours.

For the topping, whip together the cream, sugar, and vanilla, and spread a layer 1-inch thick on top of the mousse filling.

Chocolate Truffles

Yield: about 36 truffles

Here's a trivia question. Who started the hotel custom of placing a chocolate on the pillow or night stand when the bed is turned down? Answer: Cary Grant. About forty years ago, he was staying at the Mayfair Hotel in St. Louis with his lady friend. Our manager, making a routine room inspection, found that Mr. Grant (who was performing at a local theater) had left a trail of chocolates starting at the front door of the suite, going through the sitting room, into the bedroom, and up the length of the bed to the pillow. The manager then started the less-extravagant variation of this romantic bait at the Mayfair Hotel, an act of hospitality that has spread around the globe.

1 cup heavy cream
Pinch of salt
3 tablespoons unsalted butter
10 ounces semisweet chocolate

2 tablespoons cognac or liqueur of your choice, such as Kahlúa, Frangelico, or Amaretto
1 pound bittersweet chocolate, for dipping

In a double boiler, warm the cream, salt, and butter together. Add the semisweet chocolate and stir in until melted. Stir in the cognac or liqueur, remove the mixture from the heat, and let it cool to room temperature.

Using a melon-ball scoop, scoop out the cooled chocolate mixture into balls, and place them on a baking sheet. Cover the truffle balls with plastic wrap and refrigerate them for 1 hour.

Melt the bittersweet chocolate in a double boiler, taking care not to overheat it. Remove the truffles from the refrigerator. Spearing them on a fork, dip the truffles one at a time into the melted chocolate, covering them completely. Set the truffles to cool on a cookie sheet covered with parchment paper.

Mexican Brownies

Yield: 24 brownies

These are the undisputed champion brownies of the Known World. Alas, no one here really remembers why we named them after Mexico!

Brownies

4 ounces semisweet chocolate
1 cup unsalted butter
4 medium eggs
2 cups sugar

$^1/_2$ teaspoon salt
1 teaspoon vanilla extract
1 cup all-purpose flour

Filling

$^1/_2$ cup unsalted butter
4 cups powdered sugar
$^1/_4$ cup cream

$^1/_4$ cup sherry
1 cup finely minced pecans

Topping

6 ounces chocolate chips
3 tablespoons water

$^1/_4$ cups unsalted butter

Preheat the oven to 325°F. Grease a jelly roll pan and dust it with flour.

To prepare the brownies, melt the semisweet chocolate and butter in a double boiler and let the mixture cool. Whisk the eggs until they lighten in color, and gradually whisk in the sugar. Beat in the chocolate mixture, salt, vanilla, and flour and, once the ingredients are combined, beat for 1 minute longer. Pour the mixture into the prepared pan and bake in the preheated oven for 30 minutes. Remove the pan from the oven and let it cool.

To prepare the filling, beat the butter until it is soft and then whisk in the powdered sugar. Add the cream and sherry, and beat until the mixture is light and fluffy. Add the nuts and stir well. Spread the mixture over the cooled brownies and chill in the refrigerator.

To prepare the topping, melt the chocolate chips with the water and butter in a double boiler. Stir well and spread the mixture over the top of the filling. Cool in the refrigerator before cutting or serving.

Heaven in a Cup
Yield : 1 cocktail

This is the ultimate coffee cocktail. The hazelnuts in the Italian Frangelico liqueur taste wonderful with the equally aromatic, orangey Grand Marnier, the Irish Cream, and the coffee.

$^1/_3$ ounce (2 teaspoons) **Frangelico liqueur**
$^1/_3$ ounce (2 teaspoons) **Grand Marnier liqueur**
$^1/_3$ ounce (2 teaspoons) **Bailey's Irish Cream liqueur**
$^3/_4$ cup hot coffee
Whipped cream

Place the Frangelico, Grand Marnier, and Irish Cream in a brandy snifter. Add the coffee and top with whipped cream.

Pumpkin and White Chocolate Barcos

Yield: 12 servings

This is a seasonal dessert that is perfect for the holidays. In Spanish, the word *barco* means boat. We use three-inch boat-shaped molds for this recipe but almost any shallow mold will do. Note that the white chocolate *ganache* should be chilled overnight.

White Chocolate Ganache

1 cup heavy cream
4 tablespoons unsalted butter

4 ounces grated white chocolate

Crust

1/2 cup unsalted butter, softened
1/2 cup powdered sugar

2 cups all-purpose flour
1/4 teaspoon ground nutmeg

Filling

3/4 cup heavy cream
1/2 vanilla bean, split lengthwise and scraped with a knife to release more flavor
2 whole eggs

2 egg yolks
1/4 cup sugar
1/2 cup pumpkin purée
Juice of 1 orange

Raspberry Sauce   Yield: about 2 1/2 cups

1 1/2 pints fresh (or frozen) raspberries
1/4 cup sugar

2 tablespoons Port
Juice of 1/2 orange
1/4 cup water

To prepare the ganache, bring the cream and butter to a boil in a saucepan. Place the white chocolate in a mixing bowl, pour the cream mixture over it, and stir until the chocolate is melted. Chill the mixture in the refrigerator overnight.

Preheat the oven to 300°F.

To prepare the crust, blend the butter, sugar, flour, and nutmeg together. Divide the dough into 12 pieces and press 1 piece into each of 12 shallow, 3-inch-long, boat-shaped molds. Set the molds aside on a baking sheet while the filling is being prepared.

To prepare the filling, bring the cream to a boil in a large saucepan with the vanilla bean. Remove the cream from the heat. In a separate bowl, blend the eggs, egg yolks, sugar, pumpkin, and orange juice together. Add this mixture to the boiled cream and discard the vanilla bean. Return the pan to a high simmer while stirring the mixture constantly until it thickens. Ladle the mixture into the molds and bake them in the oven for about 45 minutes or until the filling is set. Let the barcos cool and then chill them in the refrigerator.

Meanwhile, prepare the raspberry sauce. Purée 1 pint of the raspberries with the sugar, Port, orange juice, and water until the mixture is smooth. Strain the purée.

Spoon the sauce onto serving plates. Unmold the chilled barcos and place one on each plate. Whip the ganache into stiff peaks, place it in a pastry bag, and pipe some over each dessert. Garnish the servings with the remaining ½ pint raspberries.

❖❖❖❖❖❖❖

Triple Lift
Yield : 1 cocktail

Santa Fe lies beneath the Sangre de Cristo mountains that form part of the Rockies, and on the edge of the high desert of the Southwest where the winters can sometimes be cold and snowy. This drink is the perfect pick-me-up to take the chill out of any day.

1 single-serving package (2 tablespoons) hot cocoa mix
¼ cup hot coffee
¼ cup warmed brandy
Whipped cream

In a brandy snifter, dissolve the cocoa mix in the coffee. Add the brandy, and top with whipped cream.

❖❖❖❖❖❖❖

Lemon Custard Tart

Yield: 10 to 12 servings

The success of this recipe depends entirely on the quality of the lemons. Try to find Meyer lemons, which have an intense flavor. Although they cost more, the results make the expense worthwhile. When peeling lemons for the zest, be sure to discard all of the white pulp or pith.

Sugar Dough

1 cup unsalted butter	*2¹/₂ cups all-purpose flour*
¹/₂ cup sugar	*Pinch of salt*

Lemon Custard

1 cup unsalted butter, melted	*5 large eggs*
1³/₄ cups powdered sugar, sifted	*Zest and juice of 2 lemons*

Fresh strawberries or blueberries, for garnish	*Whipped cream, for garnish*

To prepare the dough, cream the butter and sugar together in a mixing bowl. Add the flour and salt, and mix until the ingredients are just combined. Refrigerate for 1 hour.

Grease an 8-inch tart mold or cake pan. Remove the dough from the refrigerator and place it on a clean surface. Roll the chilled dough out to a thickness of approximately ³/₁₆ inch. Gently roll the dough around the rolling pin and transfer it to the prepared tart mold. Lift the side of the dough with one hand and gently guide it into the mold with the other, being careful not to break the dough. The dough will overlap the mold a little; cut the extra dough off by rolling the pin over the edges of the mold. Return the dough to the refrigerator and chill it for 30 minutes before baking it.

When you are ready to bake the dough, preheat the oven to 350°F.

Place coffee filters or foil on top of the dough and add dry beans to weight the dough down. Bake the pie shell for between 25 and 30 minutes, making sure not to bake it completely; it should still be a yellow-golden color, not browned.

To prepare the custard, gradually add the melted butter to the sugar in a mixing bowl, beating continuously until the mixture is smooth. Let cool, add 1 egg, and beat until it is thoroughly incorporated. Add the remaining eggs, lemon zest, and lemon juice, and whisk lightly; take care not to let the mixture foam. Set the mixture aside.

Remove the partially baked tart crust from the oven and discard the beans and coffee filters. Pour the lemon mixture into the warm crust, taking care not to overfill it. Return the tart to the oven, and bake it for a further 30 minutes or until the top is golden brown. Remove the tart and allow it to cool before serving with fresh strawberries or blueberries and whipped cream.

San Francisco Street at Shelby Street ca. 1890.

Piñon Tart
with Strawberry Coulis

Yield: 8 servings

Piñon trees dot the wide-open landscape all around Santa Fe. They are relatively small and grow slowly, because so little rain falls in the high desert of northern New Mexico, and the soil is poor and infertile. It can take thirty or forty years before the trees begin to bear nuts. Piñon trees are also used for firewood in New Mexico, and the aromatic smoke is one of the distinctive aromas of the region in winter. It seems a shame to cut the trees down for firewood, because they grow so slowly. Often, firewood sellers will claim that their piñon was cut from fallen trees — usually, caused by an axe.

Crust

2¹/₂ tablespoons sugar
²/₃ cup all-purpose flour

¹/₃ cup cold unsalted butter, cut in small cubes

Filling

2 eggs
³/₄ cup light corn syrup
³/₄ cup brown sugar

1¹/₂ tablespoons unsalted butter, melted
³/₄ teaspoon vanilla extract
1 cup piñones (pine nuts)

Strawberry Coulis   Yield: about 2 cups

2 cups strawberries, cleaned and stemmed
¹/₂ cup fresh orange juice
2 tablespoons Port

Sugar to taste (depending on the tartness of the berries)
Pinch of salt

8 sliced strawberries, for garnish

8 mint sprigs, for garnish

To prepare the crust, thoroughly mix the sugar and flour in a mixing bowl. Mix in the butter and incorporate it by hand. Chill the dough in the refrigerator for 1 hour.

Preheat the oven to 350°F.

Remove the dough from the refrigerator, roll out to a thickness of ³/₈ inch, and press it into a 10-inch tart pan. Bake the dough in the preheated oven for 5 minutes.

To prepare the filling, place the egg, corn syrup, sugar, butter, and vanilla in a mixing bowl and combine them thoroughly. Pour the mixture into the partially baked crust. Sprinkle the piñones evenly over the top, return the tart to the oven and bake it for a further 20 to 25 minutes. Remove the tart from the oven and let it cool.

Meanwhile, prepare the coulis. Place the strawberries, orange juice, Port, sugar, and salt in a food processor and purée until smooth. Refrigerate the purée until you are ready to serve.

Place a pool of the coulis on a serving plate and arrange a slice of the tart on top; garnish with the sliced strawberries and mint.

CATHEDRAL OF SAN FRANCISCO.

Planned version (not completed) St. Francis Cathedral ca. 1885.
Courtesy of Museum of New Mexico.

Chocolate Natillas

Yield: 4 servings

Natillas are the quintessential New Mexican dessert. Traditionally, a natilla is an egg custard with egg whites folded in, and this was the genesis of La Casa Sena's version. Then a chocoholic in our pastry kitchen decided to put a spin on the recipe and things degenerated — or perhaps evolved — until the dessert became almost (but not quite) a mousse. So, although this delicious, iconoclastic recipe bears little or no resemblance to the orthodox original, we still keep the name.

2 cups chocolate chips
¼ crème de cacao liqueur
½ tablespoon ground cinnamon

1 cup heavy cream, whipped to firm peaks
1½ tablespoons freshly grated, or dried unsweetened, coconut

In a saucepan, melt the chocolate chips. Add the liqueur and cinnamon and set the mixture aside for 10 minutes to cool. Fold in the whipped cream completely. Chill thoroughly. To serve, half fill a red-wine glass with the chocolate mixture and sprinkle the grated coconut on top.

Orange Chiffon Cake

Yield: 12 servings

Chiffon cakes and pies date from the 1940s. Their light texture, resembling the gauzy material, is in part the result of using oil rather than butter or solid shortening. Classics such as Lemon Chiffon pie seem to have fallen into disfavor along with charlotte russe, Bavarian cream, rum *babas*, peach Melba, and other favorites of past generations. This recipe in part redresses the balance.

1 cup cake flour
1/2 cup sugar
1 1/2 teaspoons baking soda
1/4 teaspoon salt
2 egg yolks, at room temperature
1 tablespoon orange zest

1/3 cup fresh orange juice, strained
2 tablespoons vegetable oil
6 egg whites
1/4 teaspoon cream of tartar
*1 orange, very thinly sliced and
 seeded, for garnish*

Preheat the oven to 325°F. Grease and flour a 9-inch tube pan.

In a medium mixing bowl, sift together the flour, sugar, baking soda, and salt. Make a well in the center of the flour mixture and add the egg yolks, orange zest, orange juice, and vegetable oil. With an electric mixer, mix the ingredients on slow speed for 2 to 3 minutes, or until incorporated.

In a separate bowl, beat together the egg whites and cream of tartar until the whites are stiff. Using a rubber spatula, gently fold the egg whites into the batter, a quarter at a time just until they are combined; do not overmix.

Pour the batter into the prepared pan and bake in the preheated oven for 35 to 40 minutes, or until a toothpick inserted comes out dry. Remove the pan from the oven and invert it on a rack immediately. Let the cake cool completely.

When the cake has cooled, remove it from the pan and decorate it with the orange slices.

Pumpkin Cheesecake

Yield: 12 servings

Pumpkin, which has long been grown by native Americans, is an under-rated ingredient, usually relegated to Thanksgiving and the holidays because it is considered a seasonal vegetable. It is nothing if not versatile, making, among other things, delicious soups, bread, pies, and flans. This recipe is about the best use of all for pumpkin, at least to date.

Crust

⅓ cup all-purpose flour
4 teaspoons sugar
4 tablespoons melted butter

⅓ cup piñones (pine nuts),
*   coarsely ground*

Filling

1 pound cream cheese
1 cup sugar
1½ tablespoons cornstarch

2 eggs
½ cup pumpkin purée
1 cup sour cream

Preheat the oven to 300°F.

To prepare the crust, mix the flour, sugar, butter and nuts together in a mixing bowl with a wooden spoon. Using the palm of your hand, spread the dough evenly in the bottom of a 9-inch springform pan. Bake the crust in the preheated oven for no more than 15 minutes, until it is a light golden brown.

To prepare the filling, soften the cream cheese with a wooden spoon in a mixing bowl, adding the sugar in increments until it is all incorporated. Then add the cornstarch in the same manner until it, too, is incorporated. Add 1 egg and whisk it in until all the lumps have disappeared. Then whisk in the other egg, beating until the mixture is smooth.

In a separate bowl, whisk together the pumpkin purée and the sour cream until they are well blended. Add the cream cheese mixture, blending until the batter is smooth. Pour the mixture over the crust and bake the cake in the preheated oven for 45 minutes.

Remove the cake from the oven, and when it is cool, refrigerate it in the pan for 4 hours before serving.

Avocado and Lime Cheesecake

Yield: 12 servings

This dessert won first place for La Casa Sena in a regional cooking contest held in the late 1980s. The mayors of Santa Fe, Phoenix, Tucson, Denver, El Paso, and Amarillo organized the event, but after Santa Fe walked away with all the prizes in the first two annual contests, everyone else dropped out in a fit of collective pique! The episode only reinforces Santa Fe's claim to be a culinary oasis in the Southwest.

Crust

½ cup melted butter

2 cups graham cracker crumbs

1⅓ cups ground piñones (pine nuts)

Filling

1½ cups mashed avocado (about 2 avocados)

1 pound cream cheese

1 cup sugar

6 eggs

¼ cup fresh lime juice

1 tablespoon lemon zest

2 teaspoons vanilla extract

1 cup sour cream

Topping

3 cups sour cream

2 tablespoons sugar

1 teaspoon vanilla extract

½ cup piñones (pine nuts)

Preheat the oven to 350°F.

To prepare the crust, mix the butter and nuts together with the graham cracker crumbs, using a wooden spoon until they adhere in a mass. Using the palm of your hand, spread the dough evenly in the bottom of a 9-inch springform pan.

To prepare the filling, cream the avocados, cream cheese, and sugar together in a mixing bowl. With an electric mixer, beat in the eggs, one at a time. Add the lime juice, lemon zest, and vanilla, and blend together until smooth. Fold in the sour cream. Pour the mixture onto the crust in the springform pan and bake the cake in the preheated oven for 30 minutes.

To prepare the topping, mix the sour cream, sugar, and vanilla together in a mixing bowl. Spread the topping over the baked cheesecake. Sprinkle the pine nuts over the top and return the cake to the oven for 5 more minutes. Remove the cheesecake from the oven and when it is cool, refrigerate it in the pan for 6 to 8 hours at least, until it is firm.

Poached Apricots
with Raspberry Wine

Yield: 8 servings

As the title suggests, raspberry wine is an important ingredient in this light dessert. There aren't, however, too many raspberry wines about, and the best is Bonny Doon's Framboise. Creamy, dark, and almost like a cassis in texture, it is well worth searching for.

Apricots (and other soft fruit) are grown in surprising quantities in northern New Mexico.

12 fresh apricots
Raspberry Wine Sauce
   (recipe follows)
1 cup heavy cream
2 tablespoons sugar

2 cups black or red raspberries,
   puréed and sprained
8 black raspberries, for garnish
8 mint sprigs, for garnish

In a sauté pan, lightly poach the apricots in simmering water until they are soft but not yet mushy. Peel the apricots, cut them in half, and remove the stones. Place the halves on a cookie sheet or baking tray and chill them in the refrigerator.

Meanwhile, prepare the sauce.

When the apricots are chilled, whip the cream to stiff peaks, add the sugar and raspberry purée, and fold all the ingredients together. Fill the apricot halves with this mixture.

Arrange the filled apricot halves on a pool of the sauce and garnish them with black raspberries and fresh mint.

Raspberry Wine Sauce   Yield: about 2½ cups

2 cups red raspberries
1 cup raspberry wine

¼ cup sugar

Purée the raspberries, the raspberry wine, and sugar together and strain the mixture.

Opposite page:
A selection of ices are
cupped in Piñon Tuiles,
page 191, and, below,
an individual version of
the Piñon Tart with
Strawberry Coulis,
page 180.

Tablita
(Artifact)

Katchina
(Artifact)

Studying the Petroglyphs
Marshall Lomakema

Sena Flan

In most of Europe, flans are pastry shells filled with fruit, custard, or some savory filling. In Spain, Mexico, and the American Southwest, *flan* refers to a baked custard that is usually topped with caramel. You'll find flan on the dessert menu of most traditional Southwestern restaurants and even humble cafés and diners, although they tend to vary in quality and palatability. The important difference between a good flan and an excellent one is the cooking of the caramel; it should be deep brown, sweet, and rich, and not taste burned.

1 cup sugar
1½ tablespoons water
½ teaspoon fresh lemon juice

4 eggs
3 cups milk
½ vanilla bean

To make the caramel, place ¾ cup of the sugar, the water, and lemon juice in a saucepan. Over high heat and without stirring, cook until the ingredients turn a dark caramel color (until the mixture just begins to smoke; this will take about 10 or 15 minutes). Immediately pour the syrup into six 1-cup (8-ounce) ramekins or custard cups and place them in the refrigerator to chill.

Preheat the oven to 400°F.

In a mixing bowl, whisk the eggs and the remaining ¼ cup of sugar together. Split the vanilla bean half lengthwise and scrape the seeds into a saucepan, discarding the remaining pod; add the milk and bring to a boil. Add the boiling vanilla milk to the egg mixture a little at a time, whisking continuously. Strain the custard into a clean bowl, using a *chinois* or very fine strainer, and then pour it into the ramekins over the caramel.

Cover the ramekins with foil and place them in a *bain-marie* or water bath, making sure the water comes about half-way up the sides of the cups. Bake the flans in the preheated oven for 50 minutes or until they are set. Let the custards cool and then refrigerate them for at least 1 hour.

Vanilla Ice Cream
with Cajeta Sauce

Yield: about 1⅓ quarts

Ice cream was invented by the Italians, but it quickly became popular in the United States and has never looked back.

The best vanilla beans come from Tahiti and Mexico. They should be shiny and supple, with a strong aroma, which shows they are fresh.

Cajeta, or caramelized goat's milk, is a Mexican classic. It is wonderful drizzled over ice cream, and it has a flavor dimension beyond that of regular caramel. Fresh goat's milk is usually available from health-food stores, and the canned condensed version is often found in the diet section of supermarkets.

2 cups heavy cream
2 cups milk
1 vanilla bean, split lengthwise and scraped

1 cup sugar
8 egg yolks
Cajeta Sauce (recipe follows)

Place the cream, milk, and vanilla bean in a heavy-bottomed pan and bring the mixture to a boil. Meanwhile, in a mixing bowl, whisk the sugar into the egg yolks until the mixture is pale yellow. When the cream mixture comes to a boil, pour about 1 cup of it into the yolk mixture, stirring it well. Add the rest of the cream and whisk well. Return the custard to the pan, and cook it over high heat until the mixture coats the back of a spoon, about 2 minutes. Do not let the mixture boil. Immediately remove the pan from the heat and strain the custard into a clean mixing bowl. Discard the vanilla bean.

Chill the custard in the refrigerator and, when it is completely cold, transfer it to an ice-cream machine and freeze it according to the manufacturer's directions.

Cajeta Sauce   Yield: 2 cups

1½ cups sugar
1 cup milk
3 cups goat's milk

1 teaspoon cornstarch
Dash of baking soda

Place ¾ cup of the sugar in a small sauté pan and heat it over medium heat for about 7 or 8 minutes, stirring constantly, until it is melted, smooth, and golden brown. Remove the caramelized sugar from the heat.

Combine both milks in a large pitcher. Pour about 1 cup of the mixture into a small bowl. Stir in the cornstarch and baking soda and set aside.

In a saucepan over medium heat, combine the remaining ¾ cup sugar with the remaining 3 cups milk. Bring the mixture just to a boil, stirring occasionally. Stirring vigorously, add the reserved caramelized sugar all at once. Add the reserved milk and cornstarch mixture, still stirring.

Cook over low heat, stirring occasionally, until the cajeta begins to thicken and darken, 35 to 45 minutes. Continue to cook for 15 minutes more, stirring constantly to prevent the sauce from sticking and scorching.

Serve the sauce warm or at room temperature.

San Francisco Street view looking east toward La Parroquia ca. 1865. Courtesy Museum of New Mexico.

Meringue Biscochitos

Yield: about 24 biscochitos

The noble *biscochito* is not merely a cookie; it was recently designated the Official State Cookie of New Mexico. (Such are the weighty matters of importance that the New Mexico State Legislature must wrestle with when it convenes annually.)

These are not they. It's not possible to make a genuine biscochito without lard and, because we don't advocate lard for health reasons, we've adapted the recipe while keeping the same flavor. The meringue won't affect your cholesterol level, or your waistline, so eating this dessert is almost as good as dieting!

3 egg whites
¼ teaspoon cream of tartar
3 tablespoons sugar

3 tablespoons powdered sugar
½ tablespoon anise seeds

Preheat the oven to 300°F. Butter a cookie sheet and line it with parchment paper.

In a mixing bowl, whip the egg whites and cream of tartar to soft peaks. Gradually add the sugar, whipping continuously until stiff peaks form.

Thoroughly mix the powdered sugar and anise seeds together. Fold the sugar into the egg whites and spread the mixture on the prepared cookie sheet about ⅛-inch thick. Bake the meringue in the preheated oven for 30 minutes or until it is light brown.

Remove the mixture from oven, let it cool, and cut it with a cookie cutter into about 24 biscochitos. Serve 3 on a plate, together with a scoop of sorbet (see pages 194-195).

Alternatively, they can be made into a sorbet "sandwich." Place a biscochito on a serving plate and cover it with a scoop of sorbet. Add a second biscochito, cover that with another scoop, and top with the third biscochito.

Piñon Tuiles

These marvelous cookies can be served flat and as they are, bent into the shape of a traditional clay roofing tile, or formed into a cup. They can then be used to hold ice cream, sorbet, fruit, or some combination of these. They can even be dipped into warm chocolate for a truly decadent dessert. You can omit the pine nuts if you prefer plain *tuiles* for a change.

³/₄ tablespoon all-purpose flour
¹/₄ cup sugar
2 egg whites

³/₄ tablespoon melted unsalted butter
¹/₂ cup whole piñones (pine nuts)

Preheat the oven to 350°F. Butter a large cookie sheet.

In a mixing bowl, mix the flour and sugar together. Add the egg whites and melted butter, and mix at low speed with an electric mixer until the ingredients are just blended. Fold in the *piñones*. Refrigerate the batter for at least 1 hour.

Ladle 1 tablespoon of the batter onto the cookie sheet, and spread it with the back of a fork to make it uniformly round and about 4 inches in diameter. Repeat with the remaining batter. Bake the tuiles in the preheated oven for 10 minutes or until they are golden brown.

Using a metal spatula and working with one cookie at a time, carefully lift a tuile off the cookie sheet. While it is still warm, bend it over a rolling pin or broom handle into a taco-shape or flip it immediately onto a cup to mold it, ruffling the edges in a wavy pattern. (If the cookies start to harden before you have managed to mold them, simply return them to the oven briefly; they will soften in the heat and be pliable again.) Let the cookies cool until they have hardened before filling them.

Piñon Ice Cream

Yield: about 1⅓ quarts

In New Mexico, there is a bumper *piñon* or pine nut harvest every two or three years — great crops never follow one another in consecutive years. This is probably because the piñon tree grows slowly. In fall one frequently sees whole families, having spread out a large sheet or blanket, shaking piñon trees to catch the nuts or cones when they drop. The nuts must then be prized from the cones, a task usually made easier by roasting. It is this labor-intensive process that makes piñones rather costly.

This ice cream is also great with cajeta sauce (page 189).

1 cup piñones (pine nuts)	*Pinch of salt*
1 cup half-and-half	*½ cup sugar*
3 cups milk	*12 egg yolks*

Preheat the oven to 350°F. Toast the piñones in a single layer on a baking sheet until they are golden brown.

Place the half-and-half, milk, and salt in a heavy-bottomed pan and bring the mixture to a boil. Add the toasted nuts, remove the pan from the heat, and let the mixture infuse for 1 hour. Strain the mixture back into a clean saucepan, and reserve the nuts.

In a mixing bowl, whisk the sugar into the egg yolks until the mixture is pale yellow. Reheat the milk mixture, bring it to a boil. Pour about 1 cup of the boiling milk into the yolk mixture, stirring well. Whisk the rest of the milk into the egg yolks, return the custard to the pan, and cook it over high heat until it coats the back of a spoon, about 2 minutes. Do not let the mixture boil. Immediately remove the custard from the heat and strain it into a clean mixing bowl.

Set the custard aside to chill in the refrigerator. When the mixture is completely cold, transfer it to an ice cream machine and freeze it according to the manufacturer's directions. Stir the reserved pine nuts back in at the end of the freezing process.

White Chocolate Ice Cream

Yield: about 1½ quarts

White chocolate is not really chocolate — it does not contain any of the chocolate "liquor" or paste that is refined from the cocoa bean to make regular, brown chocolate. Instead, it is made from cocoa butter, a natural oil in the bean, that is separated from the chocolate liquor before the liquor is refined to make chocolate. Some white chocolate on the market doesn't even contain cocoa butter, but is made up from other ingredients, which is why it can vary greatly in quality. We recommend your buying the best you can find, our first choice being the French white chocolate made by Valrhona; the Belgian Callebaut runs it a close second.

4 cups milk
¾ cup sugar

8 egg yolks
8 ounces white chocolate, chopped

Place the milk in a heavy-bottomed pan and bring to a boil. Meanwhile, in a mixing bowl, whisk the sugar into the egg yolks until they are pale yellow. When the milk comes to a boil, pour about 1 cup into the yolk mixture, stirring well. Add the rest of the milk mixture, whisking well, then return the custard to the pan, and cook it over high heat until it coats the back of a spoon, about 2 minutes. Do not let the mixture boil. Immediately remove the pan from the heat.

Place the chocolate in a mixing bowl and strain the egg mixture over it, stirring until the chocolate has melted. Set the mixture aside to chill in the refrigerator. When the custard is completely cold, transfer it to an ice-cream machine and freeze it according to the manufacturer's directions.

Sangria Sorbet

Yield: about 1¼ quarts

It is said that the Moghul Emperors of sixteenth-century India dispatched relays of horsemen north from Delhi to the Himalayas to bring back ice for their sorbets. Happily, modern refrigeration techniques make our task rather less complex. This recipe derives its name from the wine and fruit ingredients that form the base for the refreshing Spanish cocktail (see page 24).

1¼ cups water
1¼ cups sugar
⅓ cup fresh lemon juice
⅓ cup fresh orange juice

⅓ cup fresh lime juice
1⅔ cups red wine
Pinch of salt

Warm the water in a small saucepan, add the sugar, and bring the mixture to a boil. Remove it from the heat, and transfer it to a mixing bowl. Add the lemon, orange, and lime juices, the wine, and the salt, stirring until they are thoroughly incorporated. Chill the mixture in the refrigerator. When it is completely cold, transfer the mixture to an ice cream machine and freeze it according to the manufacturer's directions.

Prickly Pear Cactus Sorbet

Yield: about 1 quart

The prickly pear cactus, or *nopal*, to give it its Spanish name, is a surprising source of many foods in Southwestern cuisine. This is just as well, because the cactus dots the landscape in many parts of the region, from Texas to California and southward through Mexico. Most people don't think of it as a source of food, but its leaves can be fried as an appetizer or vegetable (see page 67), and the purplish red prickly pear fruit can be used to flavor many things, from tea to this sorbet.

2 tablespoons water
2 tablespoons sugar
*2 pounds prickly pear fruit
    (tunas), juiced and strained
    (about 4 cups)*

2 tablespoons fresh lime juice
1 teaspoon tequila or mezcal

Warm the water in a small saucepan, add the sugar, and bring the mixture to a boil. Remove it from the heat, and transfer it to a mixing bowl. Stir in the prickly pear juice, lime juice, and tequila or mezcal. Chill the mixture in the refrigerator. When it is completely cold, transfer the mixture to an ice-cream machine and freeze it according to the manufacturer's directions.

Conversions

If you don't live in the United States, here is a note on roughly equivalent temperatures, measurements, and ingredients.

Temperatures

275°F	140°C	gas mark 1		400°F	200°C	gas mark 6
300°F	150°C	gas mark 2		425°F	220°C	gas mark 7
325°F	170°C	gas mark 3		450°F	230°C	gas mark 8
350°F	180°C	gas mark 4		475°F	240°C	gas mark 9
375°F	190°C	gas mark 5				

Weights and Measures

1 cup	16 tablespoons	250 mL	8 fl oz	¼ inch	6 mm	
1 ounce	30 g			⅓ inch	1 cm	
1 pound	500 g			1 inch	2.5 cm	
1 quart	1 L	32 fl oz				

Measuring cups can be found in good kitchen supply stores, but here are some approximate metric and imperial conversions for some of the ingredients in this book, all of which roughly equal one cup.

almonds, sliced	120 g	4 oz	mayonnaise	250 mL	8 fl oz
bell pepper, chopped	135 g	4½ oz	mustard	250 mL	8 fl oz
bread crumbs, fresh/dried	60 g/155 g	2 oz/5 oz	onions, chopped	185 g	6 oz
butter	250 g	8 oz	pepper flakes	155 g	5 oz
carrots, sliced/julienned	135 g/90 g	4½ oz/3 oz	pine nuts	250 g	8 oz
cheese, grated	60 g	2 oz	pineapple	120 g	4 oz
(see also specific types of cheeses)			potato, grated	90 g	3 oz
cherry tomatoes, halved	170 g	5½ oz	raisins	185 g	6 oz
chile powder	250 g	8 oz	rice, cooked	155 g	5 oz
coconut, fresh	90 g	3 oz	ricotta cheese	250 g	8 oz
cranberries	185 g	6 oz	salsa	250 mL	8 fl oz
cucumber, chopped	120 g	4 oz	salt	250 g	8 oz
feta cheese	120 g	4 oz	stew/cubed meat	185 g	6 oz
flour	155 g	5 oz	sugar		
goat cheese	120 g	4 oz	brown	185 g	6 oz
grapes	120 g	4 oz	granulated	185 g	6 oz
herbs	155 g	5 oz	powdered	250 g	8 oz
hollandaise sauce	250 mL	8 fl oz	sundried tomatoes	185 g	6 oz
jícama, julienned	90 g	3 oz	wafer crumbs	60 g	2 oz
masa harina	155 g	5 oz	water chestnuts, chopped	155 g	5 oz

Ingredients and Terms

arugula	rocket
baking soda	bicarbonate of soda
Belgian endive	chicory
bell pepper	sweet pepper/capsicum
broil	grill
cake flour	substitute sifted plain flour
cantaloupe	rock melon
cilantro	fresh coriander
corn syrup, light	substitute golden syrup
cornmeal	finely ground maize
cornstarch	cornflour/corn powder
eggplant	aubergine
flour	
all-purpose	plain
whole wheat	wholemeal
golden raisins	sultanas
grill	barbecue
ground	minced
half and half	half cream

heavy cream	double cream
honey	clear honey
molasses	black treacle
Monterey Jack cheese	substitute mild white melting cheese
New York steak	sirloin steak
papaya	paw paw
pine nuts	pine kernels
powdered sugar	icing sugar
preserves	jam
rack of lamb	crown roast
red onion	Spanish onion
Romaine lettuce	Cos lettuce
scallions	spring/green onions
semi-sweet chocolate	plain chocolate
shortening	lard/white vegetable fat
sour cream	substitute crème fraîche

Index